SPORTING Chance

One Man's Journey to Take On the World

Ed Hawkins

Pitch Publishing Ltd
A2 Yeoman Gate
Yeoman Way
Durrington
BN13 3QZ

Email: info@pitchpublishing.co.uk
Web: www.pitchpublishing.co.uk

Published by Pitch Publishing 2011

Text © 2011 Edward Hawkins

A CIP catalogue record for this book is available from the British Library.

13-digit ISBN: 978-1-90805-106-6

Printed and bound in Great Britain by The CPI Group

CONTENTS

Introduction

Gambling School

Social services really should have got involved. Don't get me wrong, my childhood wasn't an abusive one in the conventional sense. My mum didn't insist on dressing me as a girl and I was never made to do PE in my pants at school.

That was because I was rarely there.

There's the rub. Dad was the 'problem'. He was the horseracing correspondent for *The Guardian* newspaper for 27 years. After such a length of time doing a job like that he would find it hard to get motivated about a slog up a motorway to some godforsaken outpost like Pontefract or Fakenham to report on horses which by the time he got home at night would be on their way to the Pritt-Stick factory.

This was where I came in. I was company I suppose. From the age of about eight I can remember Dad bursting into my room on a weekday morning, urging me to emerge from under my Superman duvet with the words: "Come on boy, Bangor today… you'll learn a lot."

Of course I protested this was a huge inconvenience, mumbling something about Wednesday being dumplings day and Vicky Smith had promised to show me hers.

I loved it really. What kid wouldn't? Listening to Chuck Berry on the cassette player as our blue Ford Sierra gamely chugged toward sporting mediocrity, studying the form of nags instead of being puzzled by long multiplication, listening to bookmakers in pork pie hats bellow in their own language rather than Mrs Thackit drone on about Wordsworth, marvelling at how I could have eye-to-eye conversations with jockeys, getting bought a prawn cocktail at Little Chef on the way home. Rapture.

The headmaster would eventually call at home to find out why I was so often absent, perhaps fearing to discover that I was having to cook and clean for two invalided parents. Or something.

Dad sorted it, though. Once Mr Moggerson found out what Dad did for a living, he forgot what he came for. The horses are the weakness of so many. Dad gave him a spare copy of 'Directory of the Turf', a few anecdotes about Lester Piggott and some horses to follow for the summer Classics. On your way now, there's a good chap.

Mr Moggerson needn't have worried. The racecourse proved to be as good a place to learn as the classroom. The betting ring was my maths class. Working out the potential return from my pocket money on an 11-2 shot was mathematics in its purest form. And listening to Dad and other journalists craft their copy at the end of the day was a masterclass in grammar and vocabulary, not to mention learning new swear words to impress my friends when I did turn up for lessons.

It wasn't always so enchanting. My English lessons were interrupted regularly at Newbury by the lights going out in a press hut which didn't even face the track. For a big meeting at Aintree there were so few toilets that racegoers would pee in the sink. If Dad's Tandy – an early laptop with a screen about four inches wide – would not, how did he put it? "fucking transmit!" his copy to the racing desk in London, I was sent out of the press room to look for any fivers the bookies might have left behind. They never did.

I can remember being dismissed to scavenge at Cheltenham on a chilly March evening when the Tandy was coming in for particularly colourful criticism and spotting another small boy kicking his heels through the discarded betting slips and half-bitten burgers. He, too, was waiting for his dad.

"There's mine up there," he said pointing to the name P Scudamore on the jockeys' honours board.

"There's mine up there," I replied, pointing to a figure illuminated by the orange glow of the press box appearing to launch his computer through the window.

There were more glamorous trips. If Dad would have to write a piece about a particular trainer I would join him on his visit to the stable yard. Once when he was in deep conversation with the trainer of Desert Orchid, I fed the grey horse a whole pack of Polos, vowing to never again wash my right hand which was covered in the snot and saliva of one of the most famous horses there has ever been. A couple of days later Desert Orchid ran and lost. I cried for an afternoon, in part because I blamed myself for attempting to give the animal a sugar high to propel him past his rivals, but mainly because I had saved up two weeks of pocket money to bet on him.

While other kids were saving their pennies and pence to buy Panini football stickers – there was a chronic lack of Oxford United's Trevor Hebberd preventing everyone from completing the set I seem to recall – every two weeks or so I would give Dad my £2 to take to the bookmaker to put on a horse which, with my blond head barely reaching over the rails, I had spied through my set of binoculars and thought 'that looks quite good'.

If my horse won I was the most popular kid in school because I could afford to buy enough Trevor Hebberds for the whole class. If it didn't I would start to sniffle, worried that I was going to disappoint new found chums who were desperate to get their hands on the equally elusive Mel Sterland from Sheffield Wednesday. But Dad always put me right.

"There are 999 reasons why horses don't win – the one you back will know all of them." They don't teach you that in school.

Gambling Life

You've heard the sort of thing, you've probably even said it: "Old so and so's useless. He couldn't tip the winner of a walkover." Every day in every betting shop the tipster is cursed for his incompetence. Like the weatherman, people always remember when he is wrong, seldom when he is right. Fast forward 20 years from the boy who blew too much pocket money on horses, I was old so and so.

That's right, a tipster and with the betting bible that was the *Racing Post* no less. But this is where it gets confusing. I was the cricket tipster. "Do they even bet on cricket?" you say. Did Pavarotti like his grub? An enormous amount.

The sound of wallet hitting bookmaker's cash desk is almost as synonymous with the game as leather on willow. Betting on the sport has grown into massive global business.

Cricket tipster was a deviation from where one might have thought I would end up given those formative years. The left-field move can be summed up with one word: rebellion. That rite of passage that all teenagers must skulk, eschewing the values of their parents to discover their identity.

Instead of a continuing fascination with horseracing I became fixated with cricket. Not much of a rebellion I grant you. Other teenagers were painting their bedroom walls black or getting addicted to heroin. I was quite happy to cover my walls with the county fixture lists and got a tremendous buzz by updating the batting averages. 'I see Monty Lynch is approaching 40 for the season'.

My interest in horseracing came to an abrupt end in large part because my hopes of growing up to become a jockey were cruelly dashed.

Ever since I met Desert Orchid it had been my ambition. I would fantasise about riding the grey to a Gold Cup or King George. My school uniform, (I didn't have a great need for it), was chopped up to replicate the horse's famous silks of navy blue with grey sleeves. With a colander on my head and Mum's slotted spoon to practise my whip hand, I would sit astride the arm of the sofa, pretending to push Dessie for the line, while shouting out at Dad, sat at his desk simmering ever closer to another Tandy explosion, with "how's my style?"

If Mum had friends round she would just say, in that rather sad voice reserved for telling people the pet cat had been flattened by a juggernaut, "he's pretending to be Desert Orchid." Looking back I feel a little sorry for her, but not as much as I did for Grandad. Genuinely grey, he must have dreaded his visits when I would force him and his rickety back to carry me round the garden while I bruised his behind with a slotted spoon.

Mum and Dad tired of people thinking their son was touched, so they organised for me to have riding lessons.

With my newly-purchased black faux helmet shimmering under the Oxfordshire sun, I was introduced to my steed for lesson one by the instructor whose insistence on shouting everything from 'GOOD MORNING!' to 'NICE HELMET!' would have made her an asset to the Third Reich.

Jungle Bunny – political correctness had yet to arrive in our backwater – was my mount and he took it upon himself to ignore the instructor's bark to 'TROT GENTLY!' and launched into a gallop. Field after field we crossed with me bouncing, terrified, on Jungle Bunny's back like a puppet on elastic and with Eva Braun's orders merely whispers in the wind. They found me somewhere in the next county while Jungle Bunny, you've got to hand it to him, was picked up at Dover.

So I didn't make it as a jockey. But I'll tell you who did. My friend for that one nippy evening at Cheltenham. His name was Tom Scudamore and these days he is regarded as one of the best jockeys in National Hunt racing.

After the Jungle Bunny incident there followed a brief spell of wanting to be a football referee, which must really have had Mum worried because I would strut around the garden, dishing out red and yellow cards that I had coloured in myself, suddenly rushing over to the rhododendrons to pull apart a couple of imaginary players for partaking in 'handbags'. I didn't even have a whistle. Gosh, I was an odd child.

From then on it was cricket all the way. Of course I wanted to be a cricketer, too. I modelled myself on Michael Atherton. Substance over style for me. Didn't work, though. That approach ensured that although no-one could get me out, I didn't have any strokes which in turn meant I would only ever score about 20. Always an impediment. The dream died once and for all when my team's coach, who was the typical Yorkshireman, told me: "Play't ball with soft haaands ... like making't love't woman." I was 13.

The path, then, had to be journalism. If you can't play it, write about it. At 17 I joined the esteemed ranks of the *Henley Standard* newspaper in south Oxfordshire as sports reporter/news reporter/ tea boy/nuisance.

Henley was a synonym for upper class. If you believe that all blue bloods are inbred, then it was the sort of town that was so posh that it could sleep with itself. A consequence being that everyone knew one another's business. The *Henley Standard*, therefore, would report every spit and cough, which made it the best-selling local newspaper in the country in terms of the percentage number of the population that bought it. It was something like 90 per cent.

The reporting was far from thrilling. If it wasn't a fete, it would be a rotary club cheque presentation or a parish council meeting – a sort of Grand Slam of stupefication. One will never know true boredom until one has had to sit for three hours in a dark and dank hall and watch the jowls of the village dinosaurs wobble on about which company should be contracted to cut the grass verge outside the church. A low point was being sent to meet a woman in one of the outer lying villages – real 'my sister's also my aunt' stuff – to write a story about her belief that a single daffodil in her garden was the spirit of her dead Labrador.

When there was a high point, I made a mess of that. I think I may go down in history as the only journalist to actually ask, straight up, face-to-face, rowing legend Steve Redgrave whether he was a drug cheat. It was like meeting God and telling him that I thought he'd done it all with mirrors.

It would be fair to say that I didn't cover myself in glory at the *Standard*. One colleague wrote in my leaving card "hope you put more effort into your next job that you did in this one". But it was a valuable experience. I learnt I didn't want the cushy lifestyle of a regional hack. Next stop was the big city, London, to write about football and cricket for a national sports newspaper called *Sport First*. It went bust within a year, forcing me to write letters to sports editors up and down the country. The *Racing Post* was the only one that replied.

When bolt-high to a stable door it was just Dad and I that were the gamblers in the family. The sports betting desk at the *Racing Post* was a brood of bettors – and hardcore ones, too. This youthful bunch were overseen by a couple of elder statesmen, who looked over the flock as if they were their own, encouraging and commiserating over their bets.

And they would bet on anything: television shows like *Deal or No Deal* and *Countdown*, who would be second last to arrive in the office, who would be last to arrive, who would lose the three-coin game of spoof to make the tea, what colour jumper Gary had on.

The culture was strong. One colleague won tens of thousands by betting on horseracing but then lost it all on online poker. Another, whose catchphrase was "Salmon Tonight!" if his bet came in, had such a disastrous month that the elder statesmen demanded that each one of us brought in a tin of food for him as an emergency harvest festival.

Things were only raucous when tipsters were feeling hunky dory. If a selection went down the only noise you heard was the hoots of derision from the reader in your head.

The poison-pen criticism could at times be quite surprising. One particularly vehement chap from East Sussex – I think he took exception to a piece I wrote saying that Arundel was more hip replacement than hip – scribbled in to ask if I could please stop writing my column when "so obviously drunk".

Correspondence of that kind was always laughed off because how cut to the quick one felt after a losing tip was sharp by comparison. Exhorting in a newspaper for some of the few hundred thousand readers to place their hard-earned money on outcome X for reasons a, b and c only for the outcome to be Y for reasons d, e and f was the psychological equivalent of a poke to the eye – it stung and for a while afterwards you thought you couldn't trust your eyesight anymore.

When you got it wrong, and a few times I got it badly wrong, it was humiliation on a grand scale. The first time it happened to me I suddenly realised why Mum would usher us into the garden when anguished cries of "facking second again, you absolute c…" were emanating from Dad's study.

This is not to whinge, however. Your professional judgement was vindicated in front of thousands when you got it right and you would have a feeling of great élan at the thought of someone, somewhere (although not in East Sussex) taking your advice and winning money.

So when someone did remember that you got quite a lot right, you listened. When I cocked an ear to such rare praise in 2006, it was from a rival newspaper to the *Racing Post*. They wanted me to join them. Old so and so was getting recognition. I had been wooed. My departure from the *Post* set off a chain of events which meant I would end the year struggling for stake and chips.

Chapter 1

Sporting Chancer

Bill Oddie. The mere act of typing his name makes the nose crinkle with displeasure. "So Bill," I asked down the telephone receiver. "Who will you be betting on in the Grand National?"

"Gambling is evil and morally repugnant. Goodbye." Click.

Hark at Oddie. To have your profession slayed by a man who pays the bills by sitting in a darkened hut, wearing more khaki than the home guard and twitching at the tits on view through his binoculars is hard to take. But Oddie's reaction is pretty common. Tell anyone you work in the gambling industry and it will be their nose doing the crinkling. You know what they're thinking. 'Why haven't you got a proper job' and 'I bet he's an addict'. Gotcha. 'I bet'. Indeed. As soon as the disgust subsides (although not in Oddie's case) their very next question, guaranteed, is 'got any tips?'

That is because we're all gamblers. It's just that we gamble with different things. For example, Oddie might be 1,000-1 to be pecked to death by an over-amorous heron but he still takes that risk when spying on it. When you, yes you, cross the road or get behind the wheel of a car you gamble with your life. There is an 8,000-1 chance you'll receive the fatal knockout blow. Take a particularly ballsy decision at work and you're gambling with your livelihood. That blonde secretary who's been giving you the eye? You're gambling she's not a bunny boiler, or worse, a bird watcher.

The reason that all of us are gamblers is ego. You don't just take the risk for the reward, you take it because you like it when you were proved right to do so. That warm, fuzzy feeling that you were correct and the others were wrong. If you were hoping for a slightly more intellectual explanation for why people gamble, with pie charts, flow diagrams and complex equations, then you will probably be disappointed but as far as I'm concerned, that's it.

To put it into context: the whoop of delight a man releases when his football or horse bet wins is not because he's just earned a few quid. No. It's because his knowledge has been proven to be greater than the bookie who took the bet. Or the colleague who disagreed with you in that board meeting. Or the person who said the blonde was a nutcase. Or the one, who, er, said you would die if you tried to cross the M25 at rush hour. 'A-ha! I lost only one leg!'

When I left the *Racing Post* I wanted to be proved right. People said *The Sportsman*, a start-up to rival my former employees, would not last. After the suitors had cooed sweet nothings in my ear and told me about the great things that could be achieved together, someone telling me I was a fool for considering leaving was like them questioning my ability. They were the bookmaker and I was the punter. Ego, you see. So I left, thinking I knew more.

Had I known that when I got there I would have to phone up people like Bill Oddie to find out what nag they fancied (I also spoke with Jenni Bond, the television reporter, whose sauciness more than made up for bolshie Bill) I would have stayed put. I mean, *me*! Don't you know who I am? The finest cricket tipster there is (there was only one at the time). Apologies, this will be the only ego-powered sentence I will produce in this whole tome, besides, that's what *The Sportsman* people kept telling me in courtship.

Less than a year after leaving the *Racing Post* for my new job, *The Sportsman* folded under the weight of a catalogue of bad, bad gambles. First was the decision to house itself in shiny, expensive offices with views of the river at Hammersmith, second was the insistence of rushing out the first edition when it was nowhere near ready and thirdly, they filled it with stuff like 'who does Jenni Bond fancy in the National?'

There were more interesting faux pas. A blurb for the racing tipsters showed a previous front page recommending a tip which didn't win. There was also the irony of a paper running out of money when its *raison d'être* was that readers would be given such sterling betting advice that it would pay for itself. Had *The Sportsman* spent some of its coffers on actually following tipsters who had a proven track record with similar publications and were also devilishly handsome (naming no names), they would have got back their stake plus 30 per cent profit.

Good fun was had by all, though, in the months *The Sportsman* lasted. The staff was hard working, not to mention resourceful. When the boss was giving his "the great adventure has come to an end" speech, some of them broke away to start unscrewing one of the many flat screen televisions, or to raid the IT department for laptops. Irritatingly, I was slow off the mark in that regard and could only snaffle a hole punch, a set of highlighter pens and enough paper to write this book.

The logical next step would have been to use some of that paper to begin writing to sports editors again. Now let me say I was fully prepared to do that. The problem was the old ego got in the way. I phoned up my flatmate for advice on what to do next and by the end of the conversation I had convinced myself that I should be trying to gamble my way around the planet.

Flatmate was usually a great one to take advice from providing that you asked him when he was in a work environment. There he was sharp, articulate and full of common sense.

He was a former political journalist who Boris Johnson, the Mayor of London at the time of writing, described, in one of his books, as being a "lethal operator", although I'm unsure as to whether any compliment from Johnson is in fact to damn with faint praise.

Away from his workplace, Flatmate was a law unto himself. It was as if he kept his common sense locked in his desk drawer and when he was safely ensconced in the four walls at home he degenerated into some sort of posh twerp, communicating in such a way that if you didn't have some sort of hereditary title you wouldn't understand.

Having shared a flat for a number of years I had been able to decipher this code. "Bah!" would be his response if you walked through the door unexpectedly. "Whooa!" if the tea rushed out the pot slightly quicker than he expected and "cripes!" covered pretty much everything else.

My favourite story surrounding this super-sharp, blithely-blunt conundrum surrounded his superstition regarding the number 13. He absolutely, positively couldn't have anything to do with it. Couldn't get on a number 13 bus, couldn't leave the house at 13 minutes past, couldn't fill up his car petrol tank with any number on the counter which could have added up to 13, couldn't write anything in his diary for the 13th of the month. And so on.

When this problem became apparent to me when we started sharing, you should have seen his face when I told him that his address was Flat 3, No 64. He also claims to collect spoons from international airlines yet despite travelling all over the world in the last 20 years he has only two. But that is an aside.

As I was saying, very clever bloke in a professional sphere.

"I'm really sorry to hear about the job," he said.

"Thanks mate," I replied. "What should I do?"

"Get writing off to those editors, I guess."

"Yep, on the case."

"Such a shame because you were all set to go to Australia to cover the Ashes cricket tour, too. What are you going to do for cash?"

"Yeah," I chuckled. "Perhaps I should go anyway and try to gamble my way round the country. Haha!"

"No," he said firmly. "That's ridiculous."

"Well, I was only jo…"

"Definitely not. Crazy, crazy. How are you going to pay the mortgage?"

"No, no I was only…"

"I strongly suggest you don't do that."

"Hang on!" I shouted. "I wasn't going to. Anyway, are you saying I couldn't gamble my way round Australia?"

"Well, look…"

"You are, aren't you? You don't think I've got what it takes. Piece of piss pal, I'll show you."

Ego again.

By the time Flatmate had returned from his job I had it all planned. I would spend my redundancy money on my flights and I set a target of £1,300 to be won gambling. This equated to two months of mortgage money, which if I hit would prove that I could make it as a full-time gambler. "Forget all this working for others," I said to myself. "I'll work for myself."

It was perfect. I thought back to my past learning the gambling craft with Dad on obscure racecourses and then honing it at the betting mad *Racing Post*. It was as if it was preordained. Every small stepping stone in my career had led me to attempt such a journey; feeling suicidal at parish council meetings, pissing off Sir Steve Redgrave, being made redundant. As I said earlier, if you can't play it, write about it. And if you can't write about it, gamble on it. There was a clear desire, from a very young age, to be close to, or at least be involved with, great sporting drama. From crippling Grandad as I imagined being on board Desert Orchid to the embarrassing homemade ref phase and the flawed reincarnation of Mike Atherton. Once those dreams had died, I moved on to try to report on the action; World Cup finals, Ashes Test matches, Olympic Games. Again, fail. But this was a new era. I could be world-renowned as a sports bettor, be pictured in the pit lane at grands prix wearing big sunglasses with girls hanging off my arms, I could write a self-help book, be a guest on Richard & Judy, bring out a fragrance (I agree, I've gone too far here). It was an opportunity not to be missed. A professional sporting chancer.

The greatest gambling adventure was on. I got the atlas out and charted my potential path, bought travel books on Australia and checked on the world map of terror to check it was safe.

When Flatmate came home, he had forgotten all about our conversation and as he stepped over the threshold, his syndrome took hold.

"Bah!" he cried. "What's all this?"

"Gonna gamble round Australia aren't I?"

"Cripes! Great idea."

Flatmate showed little interest in the maps and charts which were laid out on the table, only stopping to point at the colour-coded world map of terror to declare "this light blue area looks very safe?" "It's called the Pacific." He slumped on the sofa and switched on the television. Bill Oddie's face appeared.

"Whoaa!" he cried. "Awful man."

Chapter 2
London

You know winter has arrived when you walk past a bus and are pleased to feel the brisk heat of the engine, warming your bones shuddering from the shock of the first bite of cold for months. It turned up just in time for me to set off on my 8,000-mile trip to Australia for a betting bonanza.

London was grey and drizzly. I slipped on the wet, golden leaves covering the pavement, surely a pale imitation of the streets of, first Singapore, and the five Australian city walkways which would hopefully be paved with genuine gold for two months. Two whole months. Suddenly it seemed like an awfully long time. Maybe I wasn't cut out for this travel lark. I knew how to place a bet but doing so in a foreign country while making sure I caught planes, trains and automobiles? I couldn't do two things at once. I'm a bloke, not a woman.

I was hopeless in unfamiliar cities. When starting work in London as a naïve 19-year-old it took me two years to work out the underground map was not a direct geographical copy of the city plan. Ending up in dodgy Hackney late at night when all I thought I had to do was walk in a straight line and I'd hit Old Street was one example. And on a visit to Paris a couple of winters back, frustration and confusion with 'Le Metro' were so fierce that one of the most beautiful cities in the world was written off for good. I cursed and spat my way around the underground system, furious that no-one seemed remotely interested in my emotional outbursts. Of course I realise now that I was just behaving like an ordinary Frenchman, although it would be pushing it to claim that I fitted in seamlessly to different cultures on the back of it.

Funnily for an Englishman in France it wasn't the French that infuriated me so, it was the English back home talking about France and how cherry-on-top marvellous the bloody place was. One guidebook pushed all the patriotic buttons in me by claiming that the Metro system put London's antiquated underground network to shame. Well, I couldn't have that. At the very least its chaotic nature meant it was losing on points versus London, not to mention the doors on the trains which were handily designed so you could throw yourself out while it was moving, the dark, dimly-lit and narrow platforms which made you feel like you were walking a tightrope and ticket barriers which slammed shut with such force that it is a wonder whether they were designed by a feminist keen to see more men do the can-can. No, Paris was a disaster and having left it never to return I was all for French farmers in dispute not only burning sheep but setting fire to a few boulevards too.

It could be claimed that I had fallen into the trap of thinking that I had to undertake this gambling gambol because I was in need of a life experience, desperately trying to appear to finally be doing something exciting with my life. Was this an early-life crisis? God, I didn't know the first thing about surviving in unknown territory with no pals, no money and a gambling habit which was conducive to neither.

I'm not sure I even liked the idea of traipsing around the world's sixth largest country and one of the most deadly. Did you know ten of the world's most poisonous snakes lived there? And if they were not enough to worry about, don't forget the spiders, jellyfish and sharks. Basically I would rather return home with a huge hole in my wallet than a huge hole in me.

Nope. Nice 'n' safe was my moniker. Most go out to paint the town red. I choose magnolia. A warm brew and piece of cake was preferred to a night on the razzle in case something unforeseen occurred; like when I first moved to west London and the local gangster (I did not know he was so esteemed at the time) came over to the bar I was sat at and, as if he and I were potential best friends, said: "You're new 'round here. Anythink I can get you... know what I mean?"

"Actually a fridge would be jolly good," I suggested.

Self-help gurus are always going on about how people need to have their comfort rug taken from them but it was doubtful whether they would recommend blowing cash on a two-month betting trip to Australia when unemployed and with a whacking mortgage to pay. That was more like slashing it into tiny pieces with a machete, setting fire to it and urinating on the ashes.

'But Australia will be an adventure', everyone said. Not convinced. Adventure is only three simple letters from certain death. Put an M, followed by an I and then an S at the front and your relatives are crying in the aisles of the local crematorium.

You can stick your adventure. I was the type of chap who would go to a rock concert and although like the idea of crowd surfing, would never contemplate actually doing it because I would be worried that I would lose my phone or my wallet or my keys. Or even all three. How would one survive such a disaster? It really doesn't bear thinking about.

The closest I came to one of these so-called adventures was in Amsterdam in my early twenties. I visited with Flatmate. We thought it would be a great laugh to go to watch one of the live sex shows in the Red Light District and chuckle away like naughty schoolboys. Unfortunately I had left my spectacles back at the hotel meaning that I couldn't see a thing in the dimly-lit theatre. All I could make out was what looked like a naked bloke planing a piece of wood on a workbench which had long, golden hair. Flatmate later had to give a running commentary on what was taking place on the stage, which seemed miles way.

"She's holding a candle... she's not holding it now!"

Perhaps this was the beginning of my fall from grace. After all, there should be no reason why I would be exempt from a spectacular plummet. It's happened to worse sorts and probably better ones. A few years on I could be that man at the tube station endlessly repeating in a monotone 'finished with your ticket?' to no-one in particular in the vain hope that I could raise enough money to buy some fingerless gloves so I could look like all the other vagrants while drinking my pea soup.

What blew away the cobwebs of doubt was another warm blast of air, this time from a tube train, which was ironic considering earlier dewy-eyed underground musings. That horrible, stale air which rushes from the tunnel when a train approaches, blowing billions of germs up your nostrils, into your mouth, ears and any other hole which might be open. The only way to escape is to get on a carriage where you are pressed so firmly against your fellow travellers that you pray that some illicit thought doesn't enter your head otherwise it could get embarrassing for about 15 people.

When aboard my thought process was always the same. This day was no different. I worried about the prospect of someone blowing off rather than a rucksack blowing up, fretted how it could be that the trim fellow in the suit could stink of body odour so early in the morning and panicked over what other germs were seeping into the pores of my freshly-shaven face, ripened by the icy chill of the winter wind.

And with that I decided I would not miss London at all and took a rather Australian attitude to my adventure. "Just bloody well get on with it," I said to myself.

Soon I was in Paddington. The best of London's railway stations, not just because it managed to blend modern architecture with Victorian in a way that doesn't make you want you to set fire to the place but because it was named after a bear who liked marmalade sandwiches and was sent from Peru.

How on earth did immigration allow that one to slip through the net? Imagine it. Some bloke with a bit of that gold stuff on his hat and shoulders (scrambled egg my great grandad called it) is sitting in his booth checking the passports of passengers arriving from flight Peruvian Airlines No. 492. Passing him by as he slurps his Bovril go a woman, man, woman, woman, man, woman, bear wearing Wellington boots, a duffle coat, stupid hat and what appears to be dried marmalade on his thick, black facial fur, woman, man, man, woman… "Nothing ever interesting happens in this job," he mumbles as he dusts his scrambled eggs. "I wish just for once someone would try to smuggle something exotic." Something exotic! A bear's just handed you his passport for Christ's sake! And people moan that they let anyone in these days.

If you're ever at Paddington you can go to see the statue of the bear who, thankfully, was captured when someone fired an over-size tranquiliser drug into his arse and was then made to dance, coaxed by marmalade sandwiches, for everyone's entertainment for the rest of his days. Or you could go and have a bet.

Yes, Paddington was not only the greatest railway station because it has stories about bears, but it has a Ladbrokes betting shop handily placed by the departure point of the Heathrow Express so you can spunk all your holiday spending money before you have even reached your destination.

This was where I would have my first bet on the road. Win and I would travel to the airport in 'comfort and style' – the words of Heathrow Express not mine. Lose and it would be back on the stuffy underground, going back on the route I came to catch the Piccadilly line to Terminal Three. I had acquired £50 worth of betting vouchers from Ladbrokes down the years and thought it would be a rather spectacular way to start my jaunt by recklessly blowing the lot on greyhound racing.

Now for those who don't know much about the sport, it has a murky reputation to say the least; Vaseline being put in the eyes of dogs so they can't see where they're going, trainers giving them a good feed before a race (imagine trying to hurtle round a sand track after a Christmas dinner blow out) and far more unpleasant antics like shooting dogs which aren't performing. Mind you, I have felt like killing many a dog I had backed in my betting career. I had the dubious, but nonetheless remarkable, honour of having backed only one winner at the dogs in about five years.

When living near Oxford I would attend regularly on a Saturday night, which was not only a poor piece of judgement because of a dearth of winnings, but the track was situated near the infamous Blackbird Leys Estate. Infamous is not a word used in sleepy Oxfordshire often, a county where normally someone asks first to steal something, so it should be taken seriously. Perhaps I can be grateful that I came away each time having been given a good beating by the bookies rather than a bunch of youths wearing hoodies.

Greyhounds were responsible for damage to the relationship with my neighbours while residing in my comatose Oxfordshire outpost. Watching the afternoon BAGS racing at home worked me into a frenzy and screaming at the top of my voice "Keep pulling, you bitch! Keep pulling!" meant that the inhabitants either side of my terraced cottage got the wrong end of the stick. "I'll never bet on dogs again," I told myself as the woman from No. 55 looked at me with contempt.

This time I was confident of victory, however. I had a secret weapon. While working at *The Sportsman* I sat opposite the greyhound editor, who was not only a lovely, personable chap who would do anything for you, but more importantly he was in the *Guinness Book of World Records* for an astonishing accumulator at Wimbledon dogs some years back. He would give me a winner. Getting advice from such a legend almost made me feel shrewd and I was beginning to count my money before I'd even placed a bet. "Forget Heathrow Express, I'll go by bloody helicopter," I thought as I dialled his number on the mobile phone.

"Hello mate, I'm betting on the two o'clock at Walthamstow. Any advice?"

"Well, you've been to the track before, what did you do last time?"

"That was some time ago and I haven't been back since, an indication of how I got on... ooh the one dog is having a poo,

20

does that mean it'll be lighter and run faster?"

"Well, do you run faster after a crap?"

Thinking that I did, she was the bitch for me. Admittedly I had hardly squeezed every last drop of information from my contact's considerable betting brain but I had become overexcited at the prospect of watching 4-1 shot Good Georgia romp home in first with her rivals trailing behind, tongues hanging from their mouth not in exhaustion but in sheer awe at the speed of the victor.

Oh yes, this was definitely going to be a winning start. Yet when it came to the crunch to hand over my £50 vouchers I remembered the ghosts of bitch bets past; one was bitten by another dog during the race and limped home, another tumbled into the hoardings on the first bend and another came out of the traps backwards. I tentatively handed over just £30 to the cashier and settled down on one of Ladbrokes' red, foam-topped stools, hoping I would soon be on the edge of it, then out of it and punching the air in delight.

Well, Good Georgia came out of the traps like lightning and stormed into a lead at the first bend. She was still there on bend two, and incredibly, bend three. "Surely she'll get done," I thought. But no, she was still there in the straight. My heart was clattering. Finally I had cracked this sport. All the failed wagers of the past were forgotten. I couldn't even name a greyhound I'd lost money on. They should rename Good Georgia 'Great Georgia'. What a triumph this would be and what a start to my courageous journey.

Then something irritating happened. Just as I got overconfident, so too did Georgia. Looking like no dog could catch her, she allowed her mind to wander. To what exactly I don't know. The Pedigree Chum she was going to buy with her winnings perhaps? Or maybe some natty red shoes to match her coat. Whatever it was she switched off and was pipped by a snout on the line by the six dog and favourite, Special Gift.

I admonished myself. "Of course! The gifted always beat the good. How come you didn't spot that patently obvious clue in the name?" And with that off I slumped to the hot and breathless underground to catch more than a tube. Bird flu or something equally nasty. "Never, ever, ever will I bet on greyhounds again," I sniffled.

Distance travelled: 15km
Won: £0
Lost: £30
Profit/loss: -£30
Target: £1,300

Chapter 3

Singapore

When I stepped from the minibus outside the Albert Court
Hotel late in the afternoon I was fooled into thinking that the
blast of heat I felt was the engine. It was not. It was 35°C and the
heat was on in every respect.

Albert Court, although sounding like a place where Eastbourne
residents go to die, looked rather swish, at least with a first casual
glance. There was marble, the obligatory virile-green pot plants,
a water feature – always a fool's gold signpost of decadence –
and staff in smart blazers, poised to officiate at Wimbledon it
seemed. Had I been forced to take stairs to my room I would
have bounded my way up, in spite of the debilitating effects of the
12-hour flight. A shower was craved to rinse the grime that one
produces after stewing in one's own juices during transit. I took
the escalator, a calming final journey to bring to an end the hectic
trek from London. At this point you may begin to raise concerns
about the sort of plush establishment I had booked myself into.
'Who does he think he is? Judith Chalmers? This is supposed
to be a rags tale.' Panic not. Although Albert Court was firmly
mid-range in hotel pricing options I had managed to secure a
crazy-bonkers-half-price deal by virtue of those kind sorts at
Singapore Air. I was making at least a £30 saving, which may
sound like small fry but over the course of a two-month betting
extravaganza it could prove a lifesaver – in Australia that could be
food for three days or a stake for a wager to pull me back from a

dark financial and psychological abyss.

Room 313, my quarters for two nights, was like every other hotel room I had ever stayed in. It amazed me that I had flown halfway round the world and there was nothing in the room to distinguish that fact. No quirks. No gadgets. Nothing. It could have been a hotel room in Birmingham, Leeds or Manchester; the watercolour by the drop out art school student, the slacked-back chair which causes sciatica, the hair dryer to burn your skin from a thousand paces and the mahogany cabinet designed so you can't find the television inside it, until you work out it rolls satisfyingly forward on coasters, jutting into the room so when you get up in the middle of the night for a wee and slam into it, you splinter six ribs. The only thing I noticed which set it apart from other hotels was a smear of red on the wall. It looked like blood. I was pretty sure it was blood. Someone could have been murdered horribly the night before and in the clean-up a bit had been missed. Or the last guest could have had a nosebleed following a collision with the telly and, struggling to lay hands on a tissue, thought 'Nah, I'll just use the wall'. On a positive note there was plenty of free soap, shampoo and shower gel. A saving of about £4.

Before showering, it was necessary to indulge in the hotel ritual of stripping down to one's pants, scattering clothes to all four corners – a sort of territory marking exercise – and lie on the bed munching the complimentary biscuits so crumbs collected in the navel. CNN was on the goggle box with a show about the Troubles in Northern Ireland. Briefly pondering what an awful state one could find oneself in if UVF treatment was confused with IVF treatment, I was excited by the potential for more rich confusables that are thrown up by different cultures and set about preparing myself to wander the streets.

I did not expect to do much punting in Singapore, least of all because it's a tough hobby to keep up in a city which at the time had only just lifted a four-decade ban on casinos and I had missed the Singapore Gold Cup at the Turf Club by five days. It seemed odd that a place which had a reputation for casting off its stuffy old colonial past to attract more tourists had shunted gambling in such a way.

There was strong opposition to the government awarding a licence to build just one casino, which planned man-made lakes, fake ten-storey waterfalls, a football stadium-cum-hotel and, of course, a wedding chapel. A second was expected to follow. If you think Singapore is trying to turn itself into Las Vegas then you would be right. With the opening of such a resort the government hoped to double visitor arrivals to 17 million by 2015 and triple tourism spending to \$19.2 billion.

Some were impatient for the casinos to begin. Just before I arrived the Senegal consulate was busted for operating as an illegal gambling house, pulling in up to 100 enthusiasts a night. Three of its meeting rooms had baccarat tables and the fourth was being used as a bedroom. The honorary consul, whose only role was to handle visa requests, insisted he knew nothing about the den, a tough story to believe because anyone who has dealt with such officials will know they are the most anal people alive and don't miss a trick, let alone an illegal gambling den just over their right shoulder.

The layout of Singapore and its foundation-stone success as a commercial hub of the British Empire had much to do with gambling, albeit somewhat tenuously. But to hell with that, this is a book about betting so we'll leverage anything. When Singapore became a British colony in 1818 after the British East India Company sat down with the locals for some tea and a chat – 'probably best hand it over chaps, you might have heard our navy's a bit tasty'– William Farquhar, a Scot, was made governor. Farquhar was given instructions by Sir Stamford Raffles, a big noise in the East India Company, about how to run the show. But old Farquhar saw things differently and instead of implementing these plans so best to allow Singapore to thrive, concentrated on having a high old time, sorting out his Eurasian mistress to the tune of six children and allowing gambling and slavery to flourish.

To say Raffles was farquhad off with Farquhar would have been an understatement. He believed Singapore should have been more prosperous than it was and was furious that gambling and slavery were tarnishing its prospects – although bear in mind here that historians reckoned that it did not take much to upset a bloke who, because of his short stature, suffered from angry little man syndrome. Raffles are rarely fair, you know. Anyway, Raffles sailed from his base in Bencoolen and upon arrival sacked Farquhar, banned gambling and slavery and set about reordering the city to stunt the growth of both. The result was a grid system with the city segregated into four areas – European town for traders, Eurasians and rich Asians, China town for the Chinese, Little India for... come on, I'm not explaining them all and, finally, Kampong Glam for whoever was left.

Farquhar and Raffles spent the next few years furiously trying to discredit each other and claiming that they were responsible for founding Singapore. Between them they produced nearly 40,000 words on why one was better than the other. It was playground stuff really. Raffles was the better name caller, though, which is why in Singapore the only street named after Farquhar was bulldozed yonks ago while Raffles has six schools, two hotels, one museum and one hospital named in his honour not to mention the train stations, boulevards, roads and quays. If that was Raffles having the last laugh, Farquhar allowed himself something of a solitary snigger. He lived for 13 years longer than his nemesis and when Raffles died, he was denied burial at St Mary's in Hendon because the vicar's family had profited from the slave trade that he had opposed.

Albert Court was in the fourth quarter – Kampong Glam. It was a short walk to Bugis Street market, a dense and disorientating place which tourists visited regularly to get lost among its narrow alleys. More than 600 stalls jammed themselves between Waterloo and Victoria streets. Every twist and turn looked the same and the array of goods to assault the senses was bewildering. The king and queen of Indonesian fruit, durian and mangosteen, provided much of the colour stacked high and wide on stalls, the noise of customers jabbering for a deal with stall holders was unceasing and every few steps a new whiff tickled the nostrils; pancake oysters, roasted duck, chilli crab, chicken rice and rojak.

The market was named after the Bugis people, who centuries ago had sailed from distant lands and fought with indigenous tribes so they could set up trading posts. They were such fierce fighters that they were feared all over Indonesia and the name Bugis entered the English language, infamously, in the form of 'Beware of the Boogieman'. So feel confident to continue to warn your kids with the well-worn phrase, it is accurate if only for the boogieman not wanting to 'get' them, merely just wanting to set up a stall in their bedroom.

Having somehow negotiated my way out of the market, (there were only three exits), I walked up towards Orchard Road, the most well-known Singapore street. On the way I spotted about 200 people gathered around four locals playing Mexican guitar music and a similar crowd gawping at a bloke who was writing posters with his foot whilst doing a handstand. Ask yourself how he discovered that was his gift. "Mum, are you sure I don't look ridiculous?"

As well as being easily tickled, most of the crowd were united in a common bond. They were on their way to Orchard Road. There are 69 shopping malls in the city, and most of them could be found there. If Bugis Street was the charming, olde worlde experience which gave one a worldly-wise feeling that one had just witnessed something culturally defining then Orchard Road was the complete opposite. It could have been any main shopping thoroughfare in the world. The same stores selling the same shiny gifts in unimaginative-named malls called Plaza or Towers.

Orchard Road took its name from the orchards and plantations that existed there until a disease took hold in the early 1900s and everything was killed off in the space of a year. There is a different virus in town now, however – the shopping bug. It strikes when setting foot on Orchard Road, the pulsating electric shop signs flicking a switch in the brain turning ordinary people into salivating bargain hunters. Such was the throng as I walked down the stretch, shoppers, followed by boxes and bags of goods, were tumbling out of the stores on to the pavements below with their fellow victims stepping over their bodies as if it was the most natural thing in the world.

This was not to decry these people you understand. Gambling and shopping, of course, are comfy bedfellows. Both are compulsive conditions which the sufferer believes makes them feel better and helps relieve stress. Prior to handing over the cash, the victim may well often be accompanied by an almost euphoric state about what their money will earn them followed by a depression sparked about how much they have spent. Shame, guilt and remorse are not far behind. There are statistics which suggest that compulsive shopping is a greater problem than compulsive gambling. At least two per cent of a population of 60 million in the UK cannot go to Waitrose without trying to buy the whole store while 'only' 600,000 wouldn't be even thinking about going to the supermarket because they were too busy in the bookies.

Instead of joining the thousands swarming to satisfy their materialistic craving, I was quite happy just feeling shame, guilt and remorse over poor purchases with the bookmakers and was only there to find the tourist office to work out whether there was some racing on at the Turf Club. The tourist office was not the biggest draw in the area and I had it to myself as I searched through hundreds of leaflets displayed in front of me.

The Singapore Turf Club's pamphlet stood out. 'It's More Exciting with Horses!', it proclaimed. What a fantastically dire slogan. Considering that they were trying to promote horseracing it is a given, a gimme, cast-iron that there will be horses involved at some stage. 'Swimming – it's more exciting with water' and 'Sex – it's more exciting with someone else' are two slogans which would never see the shine of the sun using the same principles. Ordinarily it would be a very good catchphrase, so long as it was used to promote anything but horseracing. It works wonderfully in any other sphere, except in the context of anything to do with our equine friends. 'Shopping – it's more exciting with horses' is better. Of course it's more fun. They've got hooves for goodness sake. How would they carry the bags? Oh the japes! 'Strictly Come Dancing – it's more exciting with horses!' Bang on it is. A four-and-a-half hands mare trying to dance while wearing a Karen Millen-sequined frock and the possibility of one wrong-footed move during the rumba resulting in a broken fibia for her partner only adds to the drama. Only 'Countdown – it's more exciting with horses!' is the exception to the rule and my word I have spent a few hours testing them all out. On the face of it horses making their debut – now, now no unfair jokes about Carol Vorderman – on the words and numbers quiz would be fun, but after a while 'neigh' as the standard answer would begin to tire, although I don't doubt for the first few shows it would still keep much of the antiquated audience in raptures.

"Can you tell me if there is any horseracing on tomorrow?" I asked an assistant, who looked at the shop-crazy crowds outside with envy.

"Oh, sorry I can't."

"But do you know if it's more exciting with horses?"

"Oh yes, definitely."

"Are you sure, because I've never tried it with them before?"

"Yes, it's exciting!"

"Well, thank you very much."

Buoyed by that inane exchange, I rejoined the tide of shoppers and was quite happy to be swept along, all the way into one mall. I had a look around. The buying was frenetic. There was a queue of about 50 people deep to get into a mobile phone shop, those already inside were jostling each other to view the merchandise and the few that were leaving the store with a purchase successfully completed had a look of relief on their faces, not that they had satisfied their urge but because they had survived the scrum. 'Shopping – it's more exciting with shops'. I tried to get away from the mass of people and found myself in the bowels of the mall, where cubby holes replaced the household name behemoth stores. Spice traders, a couple of herbal doctors, a hypnotherapist and a fortune teller. That could be fun, I thought. It would be good to get the view of an 'expert' at the beginning of my journey. Would he be able to tell me whether my luck would be in for the next two months? Would he be able to tell me who would win the Ashes? Would that question confuse him totally? Most likely it would and although I categorised myself firmly as a cynic, I was open minded enough to recognise that little harm could be done by sitting down and having a natter for a couple of minutes. Indeed, there was everything to gain. He could put me on to a good thing at the Turf Club tomorrow for if he really did have mystic powers, then he would be very unwise not to be using them for profit on the gee-gees. At the very least he could let me know what the going was like, if there was any track bias and which trainer had good course form.

Outside the stall was a board with reproductions of winning lottery tickets pinned to it. They totalled nearly $300,000. Obviously (how easy am I to sucker) they were there because this fortune teller had advised the winners on the numbers. All of them were from the years 2004-2006 apart from one in 1996. We all have bad patches as tipsters, I reasoned.

The fortune teller, I presumed it was him unless it was the cleaner who had been asked to hold the fort while the boss went for a coffee, was very pleased to see me. His skin was weathered like a leather baseball mitt that had been left in the rain and he grinned childishly while repeating "ye-ye-ye-ye" and motioning me to sit. I realised language was going to be a barrier when after launching into a monologue about my hopes and fears during my expedition and ending with the question "what do you reckon, pal?", his grin was less confident and he had a look of utter bewilderment in his eyes. I had managed to find the only Singaporean in Singapore whose English was not flawless. He jabbered on, I continually shrugged my shoulders as if I had a severe nervous tick and we sat in silence for a couple of minutes until he remembered some basics.

"What your name? When birthday?" he managed, which I answered. "What your job?"

"If I had one of those I wouldn't be sat here," I replied.

He didn't understand that but, unperturbed, he got out a deck of cards. He cut them and, breathing deeply as if trying to connect with the mother ship, he closed his eyes and started to wail. "Naa-naaa-naaa-tree-naa-naa-naa-fire-naa-naa-naa-earth." I sat there looking slightly embarrassed, wondering whether I should just scoot off while he was not looking. Fortune teller or not, I bet he wouldn't have seen that coming. Then he stopped, spread the cards in a circle, placing four in the middle – the four of clubs, the queen of hearts, the ace of hearts and the seven of diamonds. This interested him greatly.

"Mmmm," he said, while tapping his finger on his cracked lips.

He started typing numbers into a desktop computer which produced a program showing white lines shooting off in all directions. He said "this life map." It could have been. It could also have been an undiscovered Jackson Pollock.

He told me that if I wore pink, blue, grey, red and orange between the hours of 3-5pm I would "prosper". This sounded like he was telling me to start hiring myself out as an entertainer for kids' parties. He also scribbled numbers on some paper and told me to chant them every 15 minutes and finally offered this wisdom: "Keep secret, tell everyone and you lose luck." This had to be important because he repeated it twice. He needn't have worried. To sum up, according to this fountain of knowledge, all I would have to do for good luck on my journey was dress in a clown's costume while shouting random numbers every 15 minutes. Even if I had gone round telling people this was the way to "prosper" I would have been locked up, let alone if I actually did it. This advice cost me $20.

Predictably I overslept on my first night, due in part to jet lag and inevitably, needing extra recuperation time, when, getting up, in the middle of the night to go for a wee, I walked straight into the television set, bruising a hip. I dressed in blue jeans and white t-shirt – stick that in your peace pipe and choke fortune teller – scoffed a few more complimentary biscuits and set course for the Singapore Turf Club. It was lunchtime so I figured if there was going to be any racing on that day, it would be taking place around then. I certainly hoped so and as I walked to the train station I was tremendously excited. Horseracing back in England immediately felt dull by comparison even if at that stage I was only travelling to the track. On the way to a racecourse back home you will normally pass literally hundreds of tweed-wearing pillocks with rosy cheeks and binoculars around their necks while debating which one of their group, who are all called either Charlie or Hugo, is wearing the brightest coloured socks. On Waterloo Street there were two white-haired old men with purses hung around their necks with string and creating a hubbub haggling over the price of dragon fruits with a portly stallholder. And none of them were wearing any socks.

The Turf Club was in Kranji, a 20-minute ride on the Mass Rapid Transit system, Singapore's underground. It was preposterously clean and efficient. Trains arrived and departed when the electronic display said they would – a novelty for a London dweller - and there was not a piece of rubbish to be found on either the platform or carriage. Mind you, if there was the sort of fine handed out for littering as there was for stepping over the yellow line, painted exactly 70cm from the edge, which runs the length of platforms at stations, then that is not surprising – it was a whopping $500. It is the sort of obscure law which could absolutely ruin some poor tourist's holiday and I was grateful to my guidebook for warning me otherwise my aspirations of turning a profit would have been virtually over before even the first leg of my journey had begun.

On board the train, which had the agreeable buzz that all light rail systems seem to have, I read my 'It's More Exciting With

Horses' leaflet. To be honest, it actually sounded pretty exciting. It told me that the course had been built in 1999 and had a four-storey grandstand, which accommodated 30,000 fans, with a roof shaped to reflect 'the powerful image of a horse in motion'. There was also a glass-sided horsewalk, which went underneath the grandstand and connected the parade ring to the race track. Treading carefully, I exited Kranji station which was right next to the Turf Club. The entrance to the course was in keeping with some of the posh statements of the leaflet.

Three silhouettes of horses in battle, coloured gold, silver and bronze, hung high and huge above the turnstiles, which led me to a walkway to the grandstand. There were 20 or 30 men who had also got out at Kranji station and paid the $3 to see the action. They had quickened their stride towards their Mecca in a way that Orchard Shoppers would if there was room.

They joined a crowd of what must have been about one thousand-strong in the lower grandstand, studying the form from their newspapers while standing around on cream-coloured tile flooring or sitting on the yellow and orange plastic seats which were dotted around the hall. Everyone else was eyeing the bank of television screens fixed to one wall or queuing to use the self-service betting kiosks where you could insert a bank card and use touch-screen technology to place a bet. Towards the front of the hall was floor to ceiling glass with a view of the track. I decided to watch the first race sat outside.

To my bewilderment I was the only one out there taking in the spectacular view. The course looked as though it had been dug out in a bowl shape from surrounding woodland, so the trees which survived framed it nicely. Football-style floodlights reached for the sky and I reckoned that when they were in use, it was rather a special sight. Yet I could still not spot any of my fellow racegoers. Nor for that matter could I see any horses in the flesh. They had to be somewhere because I could see them on the huge television screen in front of me preparing to enter the stalls. I figured that the starting stalls must be out in the country somewhere, perhaps behind the large TVscreen which blocked out half of the track.

When I saw the horses hurtle out of the stalls on the screen and were nowhere to be seen on the course, I knew something was not right. A minute or so later I watched the race to its conclusion on television, the horses passing the post to the sound of a distant racket in the lower grandstand. And I checked again that my eyes were not deceiving me by looking at the winning post about 100 yards away. Definitely no horses.

Up I got from my seat to find out what was going on, finding an official-looking sort of chap on the second floor, who stopped me from entering another hall where more punters were standing around – looking at the form and watching television.

"Where are the horses?" I said.

"No racing here today, sir," he replied.

"But what are these people watching?"

"Downstairs people are watching racing from Perak in South Africa and up here they are watching racing from Hong Kong but you'll have to pay five dollars to join them... sir."

A sense of confusion was replaced by admiration for these people – there was easily another 1,000 watching the Hong Kong racing – who had not only paid for the privilege to come and watch races on television, but to bet on it, too. That was until I remembered the leaflet.

Indignant, I spluttered to my blazer-wearing informer "But your leaflet," waving it in his face, "'It's More Exciting With Horses!' Need I point out to you that there bloody aren't any?"

"Not today sir," he said calmly. "But on Fridays, Saturdays and Sundays ..."

I wandered off to the paddock in a vain hope to see an example of the specimens that had drawn such a crowd and then to the much-hyped horsewalk to press my nose against the glass, looking forlornly at the void like a schoolkid does at a zoo when an exotic creature refuses to come out of its hideaway. Really there was no need to get down, though, because I could still have the odd wager – a sort of warm-up for the challenges ahead. A flexing of the money muscles, especially as we were now in the twitching hours of three to five, the prime time to prosper, according to the fortune teller at least. Let's see if he got something right.

I rejoined the crowd in the hall of the lower grandstand to observe a couple of races, hoping to spot something which could entice me to have a wager, for my knowledge of South African racing was non-existent. The first thing I noticed was how deathly silent everyone was until the final few strides of a race, when suddenly my fellow spectators burst into a sort of jabbering in unison, sounding like a great flock of birds and only taking time out from their squawking to have a good spit on the floor. Silence would fall again when the replay was shown with the din returning in the last throes. After about four or five replays this got a bit annoying. When the final placings were announced it went quiet again, which suggested I was not in the minority in terms of knowing what was going on. The second thing I noticed was that the standard of racing was appalling. None of the horses had any speed whatsoever. They were out of the stalls with a gallop but from then on they just got slower and slower. I had never seen anything like it. There was no quickening of pace. It was as if they were running in glue, which is what most of them would end up being made into.

With no hints or tips uncovered I decided to pick my horses in the way that a half-wit might: on the name. There was an element of method, however. Looking through a discarded race card I noticed that there were an awful lot of horses – seven altogether – with 'Dragon' in their names so with none of them successful at that stage, on the law of averages, one had to win. Stakes were limited to $20 a pop because, after all, this was only a warm-up, a pre-season friendly, a golfer practising his swing, you get the picture. Kiss of the Dragon – what a fine name – was off first. He – I think it was male anyway – was carrying less weight than any other animal, a positive for the form was as random as anything else in the race. Kiss of the Dragon was out in front until the business end when the jockey asked it some questions. He got a similar response as I did when asking Mystic Ming about my future prospects. He didn't have any. No matter, for Speedy Dragon – an altogether better name – was next in race nine, the 4.55 and my final bet because of the 5pm cut-off time for bon chance. This horse had improved by six places from three races ago to come second in its last outing and the only drawback it seemed to have were that its colours were yellow and black, which were not in my 'lucky' list. From the off it was middle of the field … middle of the field … middle of the field … back of the field … then last and will go down in the memory bank as the only horse I had seen which genuinely appeared to have a reverse gear.

Despite the early setback of no live racing and two fun bets going down, I was thoroughly pleased with my day. After all, I had discovered that there was a hardcore in Singapore who were prepared not only to have a cheeky punt, but to pay for the privilege. And on racing that was not live. Perhaps the slogan should have read 'It's More Exciting without Horses!' To be sure this event convinced me that Singapore could, one day, be a hotbed of gambling activity. Let's think about it. We know that there is an addiction to the adrenalin rush of shopping and we know that it doesn't take much to captivate, or hook, the locals. The Mexican guitar players, the oddball drawing posters with his foot and the crush at the mobile phone store. Very easily pleased. Just imagine what the reaction will be when Singaporeans can go for a night at the casino and experience the thrill of rolling the dice on the craps table, playing 21 or watching the ball hop, skip and jump around the roulette wheel?* Raffles will probably be doing likewise in his grave.

I got back on the MRT, still holding my racecard as a souvenir. Reading through it again there were a multitude of horses with similar names, which exposed my foolishness at the fascination with Dragon. There were also seven horses running that day with 'Joker' in their names. I felt a little bit like one as I wondered whether I really should buy that clown outfit, until the comforting murmur and sway of the train and the debilitating effects of the flight saw me slip off into slumber to dream about something which I knew how to bet on: the Ashes.

Distance travelled: 10,862km
Won: £0
Lost: £50
Profit/loss: -£50
Target: £1,300

*Singapore's first casino opened in February 2010, the government taking steps to try to ensure gambling does not get out of control. According to Reuters, locals have to pay an entrance fee of US$70. Further restrictions include a bar on entry to anyone under 21, a ban on bank cash machines on the casino floor and a blacklist of gamblers with a known addiction problem.

Chapter 4
Brisbane

There were few signs of Ashes fever sweeping through Brisbane, Australia's third-largest city and capital of Queensland, when I arrived at a bustling Central Station.

Apart from an advert on the side of a bus, which featured Ricky Ponting and co standing around in their Baggy Green caps as if they are waiting for a, er, bus, you wouldn't have even known the biggest ever Test series was about to begin.

Come on, where were the Aussies baiting me about a whitewash? I tried to start some banter with a shop assistant. "I'm here for the Ashes." "I'm not," came the reply.

I checked into my hostel, the Palace Backpackers on Edward Street, chosen for its £22 a night charge so not to eat into much-needed betting funds. It was a huge building with a theatre-esque frontage and one of those old-fashioned lifts with an iron grate for a door. As I got in to make my way to the fourth floor of five the grate slammed into my left calf. Ping! Fourth floor. Clunk! It slammed into my right arm. I'd only been in Australia a couple of hours, hadn't even had a bet and had nearly lost an arm and a leg. Such injuries would be a blessing, however, compared to the fate which could befall me for a loss of concentration when clambering into my top bunk. A metal ceiling fan rotated viciously about a yard away.

On the bottom bunk was a German called Lars, who looked as though he would have made a good Stormtrooper, particularly when he told me in his broken English he had been in the army and served in Afghanistan. Yet in spectacular stereotype-splitting style he was now a surf bum. How very un-German.

Tucked away in the corner of the five-bed dorm was a tall, brooding South American-looking fellow with dark eyebrows so thick that it looked as though he had stuck a couple of comedy moustaches above his peepers. "My name is Mauricio Alves de Oliveira from Brazil." So much for preconceptions about sharing with a platoon from the Barmy Army, the England cricket team's infamous travelling supporters.

After a brief bonding session with my roommates – I took an impromptu English lesson – I was eager to discover why Brisbane had been given the tag BrisVegas and took a stroll into the city to find the tourist office. I was flummoxed momentarily to find a German behind the counter but not as confused as she was when I asked where the casinos were. She had to ask a colleague and I wondered whether she had been banished in disgrace from her homeland for an inefficient nature.

Her co-worker pointed me to the top of Queen Street Mall.

"That's where they all are then?" I asked.

"What?"

"The casinos."

"We've only got one."

"But the city's nickname is BrisVegas?" I spluttered. "You must have more than one casino to get a nickname like that?"

"Well, that's what they call us."

Struggling to hide my disappointment, I shuffled off to look at 'BrisVegas' – surely one of the least-deserved nicknames ever – and its solitary casino, which was housed in the old treasury building. From one money maker to another. It was run-of-the-mill stuff and the only aspects of it that impressed were the nearby Victoria Bridge and City of Brisbane bell tower – two options to throw yourself off if you did your dough.

Failing to be inspired by 'BrisVegas' was probably for the best. Besides there was important research work to be done for the first

Test, chiefly a visit to Australia's practice session at The Gabba. A sprinkling of Barmy Army were present, keen to have fun at the Australians' expense. And it soon became clear that their No. 1 target was the opening batsman Justin Langer, all 5ft nothing of him. As he walked to the back of a batting net, they started whistling the Seven Dwarfs theme tune. Langer's response was to flash a glance which suggested that he could be understudy to Grumpy. Langer's mood did not improve when after he received his second delivery of the session one Englishman shouted "that's one more ball than you'll face tomorrow." He didn't look far wrong. Langer was edging everything and a bumper almost knocked his block off.

For a man who also enjoyed boxing in his spare time, Langer got hit on the head far too often when playing cricket. He was Australia's top run scorer in the Ashes series in 2005 but had not played since ducking into a Makhaya Ntini bouncer in Johannesburg.

At 35 years old and with potential replacement Phil Jaques, who hit two centuries against England in the warm-up matches, in terrific form, I began to think that he may not last the series. A sell of his series runs would net a nice profit, particularly with a batsman needing to play only two matches for wagers to stand. So I did so for £1 at 402.

This was a spread bet. Now, there would be a lot of these so pay attention as I explain (or rather steal a spread betting website's clarification) what a spread bet actually is. If someone asked you to guess their age you might say 'somewhere between 35 and 40'. In the same way, a spread bookmaker makes a prediction by offering a range of 35-40. If you wanted to bet you would either 'sell' at 35 or 'buy' at 40, depending on whether you thought the person was younger or older. For every year you are right or wrong, you win or lose your stake. So if the person is 40 and I have staked £1 on a sell at 35, I lose £5. In the Langer example, if he scores 302 runs, I win £100. If he scores 502 runs I lose £100. And so on. Got it? Good. Back to the fun.

One Aussie who was impressive was Shane Warne. He may have only been going through the motions but the fizz he generated from the ball was enough to fool the batsman into thinking he had just been bowled a fire-cracker. At even money to be top Australian wicket-taker for the series he was outstanding value, particularly when I considered that injury-prone Glenn McGrath was his only genuine rival. Warne took 40 wickets against England in 2005 and although I did not expect him to repeat such a haul, (interestingly his average with the ball in England (21) was better than in Australia (26)), it was a price not to turn away from. I got on the phone to my bookmaker back home to place £70. I also backed England to win a Test for £125 and bought Mike Hussey runs for £1 at 362. Quite hefty wagers given my perilous financial position.

On the bus back to the city centre, I finally received some Pom-bashing.

"You Poms won't even make 200. McGrath's gonna rip through 'em."

"McGrath!?" I scoffed. "I could play him with my cock." "It must be big then, mate." "No!" I declared proudly, thinking I'd come out on top. But in hindsight that's something you should never admit to.

Feeling slightly nervous about the whopping stakes I had just placed, thoughts turned to being frugal. Indeed in order to continue to fund my bets I needed to look for money-making opportunities on the side. And my spare ticket for the first day's action at The Gabba was a meal ticket. Or several if I were to eat at the marvellous Food Court, where lunch – Italian, Japanese, Chinese, Thai or Indian – was available for about £4.

So at an English-style pub and the Barmy Army's headquarters, the Pig 'N' Whistle, I approached a 6ft skinhead, football thug style, who looked as though he spent every other summer throwing plastic chairs around Europe's town centres.

"How much you want for it," he grunted.

"Only $65, twenty over face value," I suggested.

"I'm not being funny, but fuck off. You don't rob your own pal and if you try to sell that 'round 'ere you'll get yer face smashed in."

"So that's a no then is it?" I cheekily retorted.

"You don't rob your own!"

Sure, never rob your own. But apparently it's perfectly all right to "smash their faces in".

The most eagerly-anticipated first day of a cricket series ever had arrived and anticipation was as thick in the air as the early-morning humidity. A crowd of 42,000 was expected at The Gabba, which would ensure the city centre offices would be nearly empty. Indeed it promised to be a day of ashen faces with the local newspaper, *The Courier Mail*, having warned bosses that employees were preparing to throw sickies to watch the action.

That was if they could get past security. In the same newspaper a list of dos and don'ts were published for the spectators going to the match, which seemed to contradict Australia's 'no worries' culture. Don't bring any bags in to the ground, don't bring alcohol, don't smoke, don't move behind the bowler's arm, don't fart, don't have a good time, don't bring any knives (actually, this one was perfectly reasonable). In fact there were no dos in the list whatsoever. The 'ground authorities' – a name almost certainly dreamed up themselves so as to feel more important – had even banned the Mexican wave, which although tedious at times, was about as harmful as a cup of Horlicks and a biscuit before beddy byes.

Gabba manager Chris Cochrane was the man responsible and he must have been a very boring man indeed to come up with such 'legislation'. "It's not that we don't like the Mexican wave, it's a great sight." Fine, good point. Don't ban it then, Chris. "But it came to a head last year where people just weren't having fun with it, they were throwing full cups of Coke, beer and other paraphernalia. It's just not enjoyable for people trying to watch a game of sport," concluded Chris somewhat gamely.

Alas, forbidding fans to use their limbs to have fun is not the only thing that had got Chris excited on those long, dark nights at home. He was also at pains to point out that the spectators would be more closely monitored than "contestants on Big Brother", a show no doubt he spent most of those lonesome hours watching. He boasted about having cameras with an incredible power to 'zoom' in on spectators. This was the final piece of evidence that damned Chris as a chap who was just not getting out enough. He used the word 'zoom' three times in one sentence, salivating at one stage "how he could read something on the back of a collar".

"Excuse me Brad, can you just use the zoom, to zoom in on that man's collar. I want to see if the zoom can tell me whether it's a 16 inch or a 16.5 and which store makes it. Zoom out again when you finished zooming in and then I can zoom down to the shops to buy one."

Still all these rules and regulations did not appear to be putting anyone off. The Barmy Army were desperate to show their support for 'our boys' as they tried to keep their hands on the little urn. And whilst I would not be upset at that outcome, I was more interested in making it a nice little urner.

The queue for the free buses to the ground stretched the length of Adelaide Street, a pretty tree-lined boulevard which was a blessing for those right at the back of the line with the mercury steadily rising. The majority were wearing the royal blue of England. So many were kitted out in such clobber that satellite operators zooming in – easy there, Chris – on Brisbane city could have been forgiven for thinking that a new river had sprung up overnight.

Thanks to the swiftness of the buses – wait one minute and five turn up at once – the flow of fans on to the vehicles was quick. So too was the journey. Once off the bus we began the far more treacherous task of crossing the dual carriageway to reach The Gabba itself. Not dangerous because of traffic but the fearful ear-bashing the police were dishing out to anyone who put a foot wrong.

"Normal traffic rules apply, idiot!" was a favourite as was

"fucking get back!" when someone attempted to cross before they had been signalled. With the police concentrating so hard on making sure everyone feared that if a car did not kill them, the constabulary would, the ticket touts were free to work without reproach. They blatantly went about their business within yards of plod and his pals and thanks to this show of cockiness I felt a sudden surge of confidence to try to flog my spare once more.

I took up position opposite to the touts so that the cavalcade of spectators crossing the road intersected us. The pro touts got to offer their wares to those on the right side of the queue and I on the left. "Gotta spare ticket, anyone want it?" I blurted in my best tout accent. As anyone who has been to a major sporting event will recognise, touts talk in an east London accent and out of each side of their mouth alternately while their eyes shift the opposite way. You don't need to be a master of body language to work out they're up to no good.

Business was sluggish and during a lull in the crossing I approached one of the other scalpers, who had clearly done this sort of thing before, and said with the utter confidence of a tout that had been there, done it, bought the t-shirt and flogged it for three times more than it's worth, "slow today."

"Can't believe it, I thought these would go like fucking 'ot cakes. Can't give 'em away," he said.

Soon I was dropping my aitches, shaking my head from side to side whilst saying "yip, yip, yip" really quickly and wondering about a trip "dan the pie 'n mash shop" when someone offered me $20 for my ticket. It was $25 less than face value, which shows how badly misplaced my belief was that I had infiltrated the world of touts. I took it and reasoned that it was either four meals at the Food Court or a night's accommodation. Feeling flush I headed off to enter the arena. A couple of paces later and I was more than flush. I was positively sweltering. The sweat was running down my face like condensation in a greenhouse and I couldn't help but wonder how England's bowlers would fare – they'd lost the toss, important news travelled fast – if I was a walking fountain after only a few yards.

It was no secret that in Australia the Kookaburra ball does not move in the air as much as the English Dukes variety, so making it easier for batsmen. In fact it swings for about only 15 overs. And it was impossible not to think that if England could not make an early breakthrough during that period then they would be in trouble.

After all, they were without Simon Jones, the master of Irish swing the last time the sides met, and only Andrew Flintoff in the visiting ranks was capable of making the ball talk as if it was a coffee morning at the Women's Institute. It could have been argued that England would have only 30 overs (two sets of 15 when they have a new ball) to do some damage. I felt a bet coming on. And the most beautiful of cricket wagers, too.

Punters share a common bond for desiring a crystal ball to tell them when a major incident in a contest is going to occur. Football bettors wish for a clue to when a goal will be scored, golf gamblers when a shot will be dropped or tennis tipsters a service break. Of course there are hints in all of those sports but there is nothing as cast iron as in cricket. It is the only sport where the rules and regulations, drawn up by the MCC when blokes had long beards and kept their trousers up with a neck tie, actually tell a bettor when to expect wickets and when to expect runs. All hail the new ball, which is due after every 80 overs in an innings.

It is a splendid aid because punters can plan their bets according to the state of the ball. If it is more than 20 overs old buy the batting team's runs on the spreads or bet against the fielding side. More often than not runs will be scored and the runs quote of the batting team will shoot up quicker than Pete Doherty. (Important: all spread betting markets are open as the action unfolds so the odds move in conjunction with what is happening on the field of play). Transversely, if the ball is new, sell the batting team's runs or bet against them because more often than not wickets will fall, and the runs quote and price of the fielding side will come down quicker than Mr Doherty again.

Despite that description of that simple cricket betting rule I considered to break it ever so slightly and buy Australia's runs before they had even faced a ball. I didn't do so immediately because I was struck dumb by two things when taking my seat in the Northern Upper. One far more important than the other.

The first, and considerably less vital, was the view. The Gabba was a picture. The lush turf such a bright green that the sun almost shimmered off it while above the vast, circular playing field, a wrap-around three-tiered stand stretched high and wide as if designed to keep eyes out which could not see what a privilege it was to be about to witness such an event. Thousands busily took their places filling Queensland-coloured seats of maroon, green and yellow like a jigsaw puzzle coming together.

And to the right the scoreboard, which would soon begin to tell the story of the first Ashes Test, yet now just listed the names of the 22 players. For England Strauss, Cook, Bell, Collingwood, Pietersen, Flintoff, Jones, Giles… hang on a second. Giles? He hadn't played for a year and was picked ahead of Monty Panesar, a match winner, something Giles has never been described as. That made my mind up. I bought Australia first innings runs at 420 for £2.

The inclusion of Giles ahead of Panesar should have meant that England's odds drifted somewhat. After all, the visitors were far more likely to take 20 wickets with Panesar in the side. Certainly it did not engender much faith or spirit in a potential England backer, or a supporter for that matter, when they were picking a man whose nickname, among others, was Wheelie Bin. Admittedly Giles had been successful against left-handers – and in Justin Langer, Matthew Hayden, Mike Hussey and Adam Gilchrist he had some worthy targets. However, I couldn't help feeling that would not stop Giles bowling rubbish and that the sign on all wheelie bins could be a prediction: no hot Ashes. With my first bet placed I squirmed in my seat, waiting for the first ball, anxious whether I had made a rick. What if England ripped through them? Surely it would be the only case in history of an Englishman physically attacking his side's captain for steamrolling Australia in an Ashes clash?

As Steve Harmison ran in to bowl the first delivery the stadium reverberated to shouting, whistling, clapping, spectators slamming the few empty bucket seats against their fastenings and others whacking advertising hoardings with their fists. A dozen swallows high in the rafters scattered, dipping and weaving in lunatic fashion, their radar scrambled by the din. Harmison reacted likewise, sending down a delivery which could have been a copy of one of the swallows' flight paths; straight for a bit and then veering off violently, going the opposite way to what was intended. It was a wide. A wide to second slip. So wide that Australia should have been given two.

Harmison was out of control, which was good news for my runs bet but not for my sell of Justin Langer's series runs. He hit two fours off Harmison's first over. The next over brought two more. The paceman was living up to his moniker of Grievous Bodily Harmison but he was only succeeding in hurting his team, his reputation and, worst of all, me. Langer's jabs and cuts continued to rain down on my wallet and my musings about him being unlikely to last the series were taking a battering.

I stewed. And stewed some more. My mind wandered to the worst case scenario. What if he gets a double century here? I'll take 600 runs now, I reckon I can take a 200 unit loss. Oooh, but what if he gets a double ton and decides to retire? That would be a good way to go out, Justin. At the top. The peak of your powers. How you'd like to be remembered, eh? Crash. He cut another four through point.

When Matthew Hayden was dismissed by Andrew Flintoff I couldn't help but think to myself that I should have sold his runs instead, a standard reaction known to spread bettors everywhere. So I went for a walk around the ground, which I had found in the past always seemed to bring a wicket. Anti-clockwise for runs and clockwise for wickets. Or was it the other way round? Unsure, I walked 20 yards to the left and 20 yards to the right, back and forth until I began to feel as directionless as a Harmison delivery. Feeling dizzy, I rested my arms on the hot railings.

Below, Woollongabba, which appeared to be a rather shabby district perhaps neglected in favour of the super stadium from which I took my vantage point, continued its daily routine. Men and women bustled in the small shopping centre outside the entrance to the Northern Stand. I say shopping centre, there were actually only three stores. One was called Adult World which promised to sell 'Lingerie, Videos, Toys, Lotions and Potions'. It all sounded rather messy. But don't worry. Right next door was a dry cleaners. Which is where Australia were taking England.

I returned to my seat and was flabbergasted to see that Langer had raced to 81. Grimly I accepted my fate. I sat back and let out a puff of air which blew a wispy piece of hair from my sight. As I did this Langer did something equally laconic. He wafted to gully with the lazy air of a man who had just remembered he needed to pick up something from the dry cleaners. I could not believe my fortune and stood to cheer Langer from the square, applauded him from the outfield louder than anyone in the ground and all the way back into the pavilion from where he could not hurt me anymore.

Soon Damien Martyn had lost his wicket to Ashley Giles, which brought Mike Hussey to the crease at the perfect time. The ball was old and England were tired. Even the swallows had stopped flitting about the place. Along with Ricky Ponting Hussey should have been able to score heavily to put Australia on course for a big total and me for an even bigger pay out. Yet with the new ball fast approaching I considered closing my Australia runs bet for a healthy profit. Thanks to the odds on spread betting markets moving in line with what is happening on the pitch, it gives bettors the opportunity to 'close' wagers. For example, if a spread bookmaker sets Australia runs at 350, yet they make 100 runs for the loss of no wicket at lunch, then a punter who thought 350 was a 'buy' can sell at the new price, which is likely to be 400, locking in profits. It's exactly like the stock market.

It would have been nice to make sure that my first settled bet of the series was a winner. Then an advertising hoarding flashed up 'Don't let the game play you. Always bet responsibly'. This could have been perceived as some sort of sign, a warning from the gods. But stuff it. 'I'll keep going if it's all the same to you, thanks' I thought and with a spring in my step I left to catch the bus back to the city.

While bumping and swaying my way back on my rickety carrier, England supporters kept everyone updated with their transistor radios. The visitors had just taken the new ball. "Fookin 'ell," said a Yorkshireman, "We can't even get 't new ball to swing."

Australia closed on 346 for three. In 2002 at the same ground they finished day one on 362 for two. A mauling followed for England.

Spread betting was once brilliantly described as "a thrilling introduction to the official receiver". You can lose an awful lot of money, but you can win an awful lot, too. That is the attraction. Cricket could have been designed for spread betting and vice versa. Take my bet as an example. I bought Australia runs at 420, which meant for every run they scored over that total I would make £2. Anything below that and I would lose £2 a run.

On day two it did not take me long to realise that I was going to win big. England's bowlers were just as insipid as they were on the first day. Steve Harmison was sending down more wides, Ashley Giles had just been hit for a six. "Congratulations Ashley, you've just taken your first wicket in the grandstand!" roared an Aussie. Then at 11.26 it happened. Australia passed 420. I didn't leap up and cheer but sat smugly in my plastic seat, safe in the knowledge that not only were the Australians topping up their total, they were topping up my bank balance.

This was one of the finest feelings in the world. Very few things go close. A nice cup of tea and a chocolate cake doesn't touch it. A nice cup of tea and a chocolate cake brought to you by a beautiful woman is closer but still not quite there. Not even the sweltering heat and no shade could spoil it. I was glistening and golden like a rotisserie chicken. Twisting and turning in vain to try to escape the warmth.

Not even two Aussies brought on to the pitch with guitars at lunch could upset my equilibrium. One song they performed was called Shane Warne. And to the tune of *Ole*! it went "Shane Warne, Shane Warne, Shane Warne, Shane Warne, Shane Warne, Shane Warne, Shane Warne!" And this proved the effect winning money has on the mind. I actually thought 'good for them. The song has taken three minutes to perform and the writing of it about a third of that. There's value in that'.

Not even a potentially irritating chap to my right could break through my force field. Had I been on the receiving end of Australia's onslaught, no doubt I would have throttled him. Every time a batsman played a shot down the leg side or it came off a batsman's pad he chirped "there's runs there". Sometimes it didn't even go for runs. But no matter. Every crack of leather on willow was like the cash register ringing in my ears. 450 kerching! 500 kerching! "There's runs there!" Kerching! 550. Kerching! "There's runs there!" Kerching! And finally Australia declared on 602. A monster profit of £364.

Back at the hostel Mauricio Alves de Oliveira was not himself. Normally at 6pm he was asleep but that night he was bouncing on his bed in excitement. Did he buy Aussie runs, too? Nope.

"Womans! T-shirt! Wet! Mens throw water! You take picture and send for me!"

"Or we could go and watch," I said. He loved this idea.

It was a good decision. There was a bigger cheer for an English girl from the south coast than when Ricky Ponting got his century. Unfortunately she let her fans down. Her challenge, literally, went tits up.

I did not have a ticket for the third day of cricket action so I enjoyed the luxury of a lie in. I was only awoken by the sound of the clock tower chiming away to inform Brisbane's inhabitants of the time. I listened, thinking it would be about eight but the bongs kept coming and when the tenth was struck I was worried that I would miss a betting opportunity.

I had to shower, dress and breakfast before settling on where I would watch the day's play. Two venues were in the running. The Victory pub, which had a beautiful betting facility to ogle and drool over or the South Bank, which had a big screen and beautiful women to ogle and drool over. Having been surrounded by men for the last two days, I decide to head for the latter once my ablutions were out of the way. On returning from a shower I found a text message waiting for me.

"KP will score big now."

Oh Lord. I had missed a betting opportunity. And a golden one at that. My fingers could not type fast enough and when I misspelt a word and accidentally got into numbers-only mode, I raised my digits to the sky and admonished them with "Come on! Come on!"

"Overslept. What's happened? Has he been dropped?" I texted back.

While eagerly waiting for the reply I hurriedly threw on some clothes and headed for the internet café in the hope that my question would be answered with the word "yes".

I hurtled down the steps of the hostel, knocking into enough backpackers to spark an international incident between the UK and five or six countries. But within minutes I was approaching the internet café and then 'beep, beep' went the mobile.

"Yes. Get up you lazy bum."

The doors to the café were opened by two floating angels and a bright light from above shone on the unoccupied terminal as I hovered elegantly through the doors and into the free seat while cherubs blew a fanfare on tiny bugles. It was a heaven-sent betting chance. Buy K Pietersen runs for £2 at 63.

Now, what do you think about Kevin Pietersen? Flash bastard, rubbish haircuts, bit good at cricket, loads of money, lots of cars, expensive pad, pop star bird. In other words, or those normally spoken by the jealous have-nots, a right lucky sort, right? Exactly. And there is nothing a punter loves more than a lucky cricketer. Kylie Minogue's 'I Should Be So Lucky,' should be Pietersen's theme tune, he could walk across a motorway blindfolded, get hit by a money truck and not only be unharmed but come away with thousands of pounds which would have been forced up his trouser legs in the collision. Before the series had begun Pietersen had five Test centuries and in four of those innings he was dropped or given a life before reaching 60. In short he made the most of his luck.

So you can understand I was feeling rather pleased with myself as I headed to the Pig 'N' Whistle, with plans for looking at beauties firmly shelved. My pace quickened as I approached and I was stretching my neck to view the screen before it was even in view. First hurdle cleared, Pietersen was still in. Relieved, I turned my back and went to the bar to order a refreshing orange juice. Full of much-needed vitamins to compensate for the nervous energy I'd be using up as Pietersen makes Australia pay for dropping him. 'What fools these Aussies are', I reckoned.

Immediately my order was greeted by a groan, which I just could not tolerate. I knew this was the Barmy Army headquarters but it was early and I could not see any signs demanding that everyone must be on the booze. "Hang on a second..." I protested to the server, who cut me dead and pointed to the television screen. There had been a wicket. The reason for the grumblings.

It will be the other batsman I confidently told myself, before fixing my eyes on the screen to see Pietersen's unmistakable swagger back to the pavilion. Jesus, he's even cocky when he's out. A McGrath delivery had struck him on the pad and television replays showed the ball was missing the stumps by exactly 6.9cm. Still, like a proctologist who enjoys his job far too much, New Zealand umpire Billy Bowden couldn't get his finger up quick enough. It was a disaster. KP had added only three runs to the price I bought at and I'd lost £94. And I hadn't even paid for the orange juice yet. It left a sour taste. Not least because Pietersen wasn't actually out – not so lucky now – but I'd been joined by an Englishman who was intent on pandering to the sprinkling of Aussies brave enough to enter enemy HQ.

"Can we have a point if we reach 100?" "You should let us win down here occasionally or we'll stop coming." "Is there anything I can do for you? Polish your shoes, wipe your arse, kill your mother-in-law?"

I don't believe I was exaggerating due to my mean mood after losing nearly £100 but this man was more irritating than cancer. He was repellent. Mash him up, bottle him and sell him as a spray which would keep insects away. It got so bad that a couple of England followers actually give him a ticket to the cricket so that he would go away. They didn't even want any money. "Just go, mate," they told him and when he bounced off the relief was audible. England were bowled out on a pitch with more cracks than on the ceiling of my dorm, just the 445 behind.

A carrot-topped Welshman took his place. Surely I wouldn't get lumbered with two in a row. The conversation soon turned to betting and it turned out that Daffyd, or whatever his name was, was some sort of betting god who had never had a losing wager in his life. Basically the worst kind of person on the earth, just behind the chap who was sent packing. In his sing-song, 'I'm from the Valleys, isn't Wales great?' accent he even had the nerve to tell me "you shouldn't have done that Pietersen bet, y'know boyo. I knew he wouldn't score runs."

"Well, congratulations then, you must have made a tidy little sum when Bowden gave him out leg before when the ball wouldn't have hit another set of stumps?"

"Oh no," he said. "But I just knew, didn't I."

I suppose my new friend also knew that Australia would not enforce the follow on and as Matthew Hayden and Justin Langer walked out to bat I asked: "Is Langer going to score any runs then?"

"Oh yes!"

"Right, I'm off then. See you."

I dawdled back to the hostel to sleep it off. When I awoke it was 7pm and dark. In the bed opposite was Mauricio's replacement. His name was Wayne. He was from Norfolk. "A've bin to the Ass-shes today. It was good fun," he told me. Eagerly I pressed him for the close of play score, hoping that Langer had been removed. "No idea what the score waz. Too much beer." What a buffoon.

So I headed back to the Pig 'N' Whistle where I enquired as to what Australia finished on. A downcast-looking thirtysomething wearing an England football shirt with GERRARD on the back told me: "The Aussies batted on. They're about 600 ahead and 170 for one. They…"

"Who's out, Hayden or Langer?" I demanded, bearing in mind that his answer would be the difference between a \$20 meal at an average eaterie or a \$5 one at McDonald's.

"Hayden. Langer's on 90-odd."

I overslept again for day three but before you get with the 'lazy bum' jibes there were mitigating circumstances. Wayne had managed to irk me further in the bar the previous night. He was far too brash for someone hailing from a county whose people were only famous for having the IQ of a Findus Crispy Pancake. He boasted that he was "crazy with a capital K" but it was quite clear to everyone that he was something else entirely although with a capital C. Crackers, of course.

Not only was Wayne galling when he was awake, he had the incredible knack of pushing one's buttons when asleep, too. He snored. Louder than anyone I had ever heard, going a long way to proving my theory that snoring was a habit undertaken by those who feel they've not had enough attention during the day, so make unimaginable noises when asleep to make up for it. He honked and snorted through the night as if he was auditioning for the part of a wildebeest in a wildlife documentary. I longed to put a tranquilliser dart in his head.

He started by making light whistling noises, which would slowly, but most definitely surely, reach a crescendo of grunts, higher pitched with each breath he took until it would sound as if he was about to choke or suffocate. You cannot imagine how disappointing it was to have to put up with this mini soap opera every five minutes and just when reaching the cliffhanger, hear him take the breath which would prevent him from dying, allowing him to start the whole performance again. I honestly would not have got out of bed to save his life if he had started choking.

So the start to a potentially fascinating day was spoiled. Not fascinating because Australia would probably wrap up the match but for the first time in Ashes history down under, I reckoned that an Englishman and German would attend a day's play together. Lars, my roommate, was coming with me. His English had improved and we were even now able to trade jokes over a few XXXXs. Spotting a huge woman wearing what appeared to be something trawlers use to catch cod in the North Sea, I pointed her out to Lars and said: "Look, she's wearing a fishing net." "Neptune!" came his reply, quick as a flash. Lovely stuff.

Indeed there were three questions which Lars could understand perfectly despite the considerable background noise on a night out. They were "where are the girls?" "do you want to go and find the girls?" and "did you find any girls?" The last one you generally didn't get to ask until the morning because you didn't see him for dust once question two had been posed. Occasionally he got mixed up. For example if I asked him what he did in the afternoon he would say, "I went to the bitch." Beach.

I was slightly dubious whether Lars would understand what was going on in the cricket, but heck, it would be jolly good fun. As we prepared to leave a still snoring Wayne behind, Lars pointed to him and said: "He make noise like zi pig. Snorker. At him I throw my shit." I was pretty sure he meant sheet.

"So we have two teams," I explained. "Australia with the green hats. England with the blue. The rules of the game are that both teams have two innings. When one is in, the other is out. The aim of the team which is in is to score as many points as possible. The aim of the team which is out is to make ten of the team which is in walk back into that part of the ground over there called the pavilion so they are all out and then it is their turn to be in. Then repeat all over again. Got that, Lars?"

"Where are zi girls?"

"No, no. No girls involved, Lars."

It looked like being a long day, not least because Justin Langer completed an unbeaten century and Australia declared before we arrived but Lars was fidgeting as if he was about to complain about wanting more living space due to the cramped seating conditions. I worried that he would attempt to invade the Eastern Lower and then open up a second front for the Western Upper. In fact, he was concentrating on the scoreboard, furrowed brow and all.

"Australia's six-hundreds and twos (hand movement to indicate a hyphen), nine also, er, twos hundreds (hand movement) one. Er, England's one hundred and fifty seven. Australia's good, England's bad," he said. He understood perfectly.

However, with Paul Collingwood and Kevin Pietersen at the crease, England were beginning to make a fight of things. "If only Pietersen had been so good yesterday", I wished as he passed 50. He crashed consecutive boundaries off Glenn McGrath and I half heartedly clapped with the rest of the crowd. "Couldn't have done that yesterday, could you?" I mumbled.

"Australia's bowler?" asked Lars.

"Yes. Australia's bowler all the time. They won't bat again," I told him.

"Okay," he scoffed as he shoved a hot dog into his gob. It was his second of the day. Before that he had a salad, followed by fish and chips, during which he actually asked me what it was he was eating. "Well, you bought it? Surely you knew?"

"It's yuk! I leave."

Pietersen whacked another boundary. I huffily started to read my newspaper. An advert caught my eye.'Gamble for the fun of it, not for the money. Set yourself a limit and don't exceed it. Don't chase your losses. Leave. Walk away. Think of the people who need your support. Stay in control.' It had been paid for by the

Queensland Government Treasury, ironic because I remember that its old building now houses the 'BrisVegas' casino.

I chuckled, pretty sure that if I had 'people who need my support' I would be desperate to chase my losses so I at least stood a chance of supporting them. I did leave. I walked away. All the way to the betting facility in the ground as Lars ordered a pizza from a teenager who looked like he had eaten most of them.

I made my way to Section 4 where the betting shop was housed, excited by the prospect of markets which are exclusive to Australia and not touched by British bookies. I was not disappointed. England's top second-innings run scorer was available. Pietersen was only 30 runs behind Collingwood and his odds were 3-1 to finish England's top run scorer. I thought about the money he cost me yesterday. I thought about the maxim 'once bitten, twice shy'. I thought neither applied. For if I believed strongly enough on the previous day that Pietersen was in reasonable nick, little had happened to make me change my mind. Certainly not a dodgy leg before decision. I had £30 on.

Lars and I left with ten overs to spare. Pietersen was still in. He didn't just hang on to Collingwood's coat-tails but pulled him back by them. Five wickets down, England were heading for certain defeat, but so what? Pietersen needed only another five runs to surpass Collingwood – stumped off Warne when not even in the same postcode as the ball – and I would have earned myself a handy £90, which would go a long way to softening the hit I was likely to take on the Langer series runs bet and the KP runs buy. Not even Wayne could stop me sleeping easily.

Nothing gets you up early in the morning like the prospect of a winning bet. I found myself in position at the Pig 'N' Whistle about an hour before the start of play and my bright-eyed and bushy-tailed demeanour was in stark contrast to some of the staff, who looked as though they had worked through the night – Chelsea versus Manchester United was screened there and it didn't kick off until 2am.

All I needed to recoup my losses were five runs from Kevin Pietersen. One shot could do it although I would prefer him to manage the feat in less aggressive style because the sight of the ball going in the air from his bat would make me choke on my breakfast. In preparation for my winning bet I took the liberty of booking myself on the Castlemaine Perkins Brewery tour. What better way to celebrate than learning how the famous XXXX was brewed and then settling down in the complimentary bar afterwards. So nice and steady KP, don't drive me nuts. Just five runs needed. You don't need to do it this over, we've got all day... oh Christ it's in the air. Breakfast everywhere, my stomach not only did somersaults but every other organ, too. He had hit it straight to Damien Martyn, without even adding to his overnight score. There's that bloody swagger again. I sloped off, head bowed. So near yet so five.

Still, spirits were lifted at the thought of forgetting all about the cricket and catching the Brisbane Air Train two stops down the line to Milton, where XXXX was brewed. I was looking forward to, as the promotional pamphlet promised, meeting Mr XXXX, one of those mascot-type characters I presumed open fetes, handed out free stuff and were generally fun-loving. The pamphlet also promised that it was 'the greatest brewery tour in the world'. That is some swank considering a lot of brewery tours, I imagined, were identical. They tell you a bit of history about the brewery, what ingredients go into the beer and then you watch some of it being concocted. The only difference tour to tour is surely the name of the booze and slight changes in the amount of hops, barley, sugar or water.

The brewery was a vast building, which looked rather dilapidated, and it took me five minutes to find the entrance. Once inside the 'welcoming centre' it looked all very swish and it really was beginning to live up to its billing, with a smart waiting area before a huge iron door with an embossed sign saying 'Welcome to the Ale House!' It was all very grand and reminiscent of something out of *Charlie and the Chocolate Factory*. Beyond that door would lie a river of beer, barley sweets growing on trees and oompah loompahs lugging great, big barrels of booze around.

"Hi, I'm Maureen and I'll be your tour guide today," said our tour guide, apparently, although she didn't seem to quite have the required enthusiasm levels. Tour guides are normally frothing at the mouth and climbing the walls at the prospect of passing on little-known nuggets of information. Maureen was not doing either.

"Anyone know why it's called XXXX?" she asked the group. Blank faces. Pray, tell Maureen.

"Well, it's not because Queenslanders don't know how to spell beer as the joke goes. The video will tell you." Maureen removed a remote control from her pocket and aimed it at the television screen before disappearing.

By her return we had learnt that XXXX is called XXXX because monks used to rate beer with Xs as to quality. One was pretty awful, four was pretty good. Did you also know that hops were discovered by a nun called Heldriigen Biggern, who presumably chose a life of celibacy and sanctuary because she couldn't cope with the shame or embarrassment that her father, Ivor, brought on the family? At least I think that was what the video said.

Maureen swung open the great door to reveal… another seating area. We all took a seat and in anticipation of something marvellous I was disappointed to look upon waxworks of the founders of the brewery, two Irish chaps. I couldn't tell you their names because the Irish accents they were supposed to be 'speaking' in sounded suspiciously like they had been honed in a Brisbane bar with too many XXXXs to oil the larynx. I couldn't understand a word. The figures did not even move so when you left the auditorium you were denied the chance to look over your shoulder and see the 'magic' ruined by the two figures sparking into life once more, going through the same bland motions and having a repeat conversation like a couple of Alzheimer's sufferers.

Now I was annoyed. For the second time in the day I felt like a mug. Even Mr XXXX couldn't rescue it. He turned out to be just an animated character on a television screen and a damn bothersome one at that. In fact I had deep suspicions that he was something of a nasty piece of work. His eyes were squinty and too close together, which made him look like Frank Sinatra, and he spoke with the most awful Aussie twang that I was surprised he didn't finish his little speech by offering someone outside for a fight. "Let's turn Mr XXXX off because he's got an irritating voice," said Maureen. Clearly Mr XXXX got his name for being any four letter word you can think of.

I began to wonder what possessed me to think this would be entertaining, when Maureen started firing facts off at a rate of knots. Clearly it was about the millionth time she had done this.

"One tank holds enough beer for one person to drink six crates a day for two hundred and twenty years, we despatch six thousand kegs a day, it takes fifteen minutes to clean, fill and seal each keg, we label 800 cans of beer a minute, we use 20 million litres of water a week, it takes on average four minutes and thirty seconds for visitors to stop listening to me drone on…"

She was wrong. I stopped listening after a minute. Although curiously everyone else seemed to be loving it. Clearly they had never experienced the thrill of a cricket spread bet if they were goggle-eyed at huge steel drums (which could hold absolutely nothing for all they knew), pipes disappearing into the ceiling as wide as that fat aunt who only gets invited around for Christmas, conveyor belts which could go nowhere and carry nothing.

The final straw was when at the end of the tour we sat down in another auditorium to view a sickening promotional video about how great XXXX was. It showed people, who had huge white smiles that could blind a man from thirty paces, having barbecues, playing volleyball on the beach, being generally matey with each other and having a great time. Of course they are! They're all pissed. God, I wanted to puke. In fact why even bother drinking copious amounts of XXXX to get dizzy and throw up? Just go and watch the video.

Maureen ended our tour with a question and answer session.

"Does anyone test the alcohol content," said a balding bloke from Blighty.

"Dunno. Any more questions?"

"How much XXXX was sent to The Gabba this week?"

"A lot probably. Ok, just sit there and I'll go and make sure your complimentary beers are cold."

Yeah, right Maureen. You're going to suck it in straight from the tap to give you enough life to complete your final tour of the day.

It dawned on me while I was working my way through my four free beers in the bar afterwards why the XXXX tour *was* the greatest brewery tour in the world. They gave you so much of the stuff afterwards that you were too drunk to think otherwise.

Indeed, even I felt chirpy when I left. After all, my quest was well and truly under way. I prepared to leave my five-bed dorm which had been more like a meeting of the United Nations Security Council than a place to rest a weary head. I had roomed with one Japanese, one Frenchman, one Brazilian, one German, one Scotsman, two Koreans, two Danes, three Canadians and three Irish. Next stop Adelaide, apt because it was the city where a fair few of the aforementioned nationalities would have landed during Australia's immigration boom.

Distance travelled: 17,017km
Won: £364
Lost: £174
Profit/loss: +£190
Target: £1,300

To be settled
£1 buy M Hussey series runs at 362
£125 England to win a Test 10-11
£70 S Warne top Australia wicket-taker evens
£1 sell J Langer series runs at 402

Chapter 5

Adelaide

They say that if you are ever in trouble you can go to the church, so it was just as well that the next stop for England's cricketers and I was Adelaide, which had 21 to choose from. The Church of Scientology on Waymouth Street was offering a free IQ test which could tempt Duncan Fletcher, the England coach, following his questionable decision to not play Monty Panesar in Brisbane while anything Orthodox would do for the wayward Steve Harmison. I too, was in need of guidance from above having received a disastrous email from Flatmate while waiting at Brisbane airport.

Hello chum
Hope you are well. Very little news here apart from the fact that I think we've got a mouse in the flat. Not sure what to do. Please advise. Also, having trouble getting Sky Sports! Please can you re-send the instructions you emailed on how to get the channels. I know I printed them off but I think the mouse ate them. I didn't see much of the first Test action (see previous sentence) but England were shocking!

PS: The scheme to rent out your room has fallen through. Cripes!

Cripes indeed. The 'scheme' was much more solid than he made it sound. A 'friend' had agreed to take my room for the time for which I was away, effectively paying my mortgage. Everything had been agreed. A car parking permit had even been purchased. Had it not been squared away, I would never even have made it so far, instead consigning my idea to gamble around Australia to a 'what if?' moment in favour of the more sensible route of finding a job to pay the bills. It was a catastrophe for sure and the immediate repercussions were to try to save more money on eating and sleeping. More pertinently, it meant I absolutely had to make my gambling target. I replied to Flatmate.

Re your PS: Bugger! Re mouse: Kill it, put in freezer and will eat when return home, that's a meal saved. Re Sky: cancel subscription

Of course it was typical that things would start to go wrong in Adelaide, the City of Churches. It was built by the Quakers and Puritans – who decreed that anyone could live there and be free to practise any faith, so long as it was Christianity – and if there was going to be any city in which I would have to get on my knees and pray because of heavy losses, surely this would be it. I felt the place had an air of reverence as soon as I stepped off the bus from the airport, a godly hush which would precipitate the crash of the watching-from-above Quaker and Puritan forefathers, striking me down when I had a sinful bet. It could have been that, or more likely that Adelaide was inhabited by some of Australia's less cerebral citizens; the wind rustling through the gaps between people's ears explained the quiet. Granted, you could probably produce a bulging file of newspaper cuttings and anecdotes on the hapless inhabitants on most towns and cities but when researching South Australia's capital, too easily I came across nuggets which left me in no doubt that the place was teeming with idiots.

Not so long ago Adelaideans used to actually boast that they didn't have an international airport. One of my favourite stories, however, involved a professor of physics at the university.

Attempting to illustrate the descent of a free-falling body (why?) by dropping a heavy ball suspended from the roof into a bucket of sand, he was baffled that the ball missed its target every time – almost braining him. Students moved the bucket when he wasn't looking.

There was also the delicious irony, contradicting the evangelical prose earlier, of Adelaide being full of places for worship and most of them playing to empty houses. That's right, the City of Churches was the least religious in the whole of Australia. Approximately 24 per cent of the population expressed no spiritual affiliation, compared with the national average of 18 per cent. This was not an example of town planning at its finest. That shouldn't stop the rest of us praying for them, however. Spare a thought for the chap in this story syndicated by the Associated Press a few weeks before I arrived.

> *ADELAIDE: South Australia's gambling watchdog is investigating why the state's betting agency accepted a bet on a horse more than two weeks after the animal died, the gambling minister said Wednesday. The Totalisator Agency Board accepted a 5 Australian dollar (US$3.75; €2.95) bet this week on Chicakaloo, with odds of 200-to-1, to win the Epsom Handicap on Oct. 7, Gambling Minister Paul Caica said. The horse was put down Sept. 9 after breaking a leg. "I was concerned to read that a bet was still being taken for a horse that died almost three weeks ago," Caica said. Punter Tom Hunt admitted he was well aware Chicakaloo was dead when he placed the bet. "I knew the horse was put down and I thought it was strange to see it in the market," he said. "So I went to the TAB to see if they'd take my money."*

Obviously someone working for TAB should have realised the horse was brown bread but in all honesty, did they really believe a punter would walk into the betting shop, fully aware Chicakaloo was no more and want to back it to win a race nearly a month after it had been shot? And at odds of 200-1? Now, betting is all about value as you should know so let's just sit agog for a moment in wonderment at the size of brain possessed by dear Tom Hunt (isn't that rhyming slang?). He thought that odds of 200-1 about a horse returning from beyond the grave, suffering no ill-effects whatsoever after being shot to death in the head and still being capable of running faster than every other animal in the race was a good bet. At the very least he should have backed it each-way. Yet what Tom Hunt found 'strange' was that the horse was still in the market. I repeat, people in Adelaide are not bright.

Conceivably there was something about South Australia's location that stupefies. With desolate, certain-death desert just a few clicks north, human-flesh-hungry sharks the same distance south and the miniscule malevolence underfoot of the Redback spider ready to sink its jaws into your toes, you had to be a bit touched to live there. It happens to the best, too. In 1983 Princess Diana arrived for a jolly and on meeting a one-armed man in the street proclaimed: "My! You must have fun chasing the soap around the bath." Oh, who am I kidding, she was hardly a brain of Britain was she?

My mind was very much my own when I took a detour from the trail to the tourist office to stop off at a TAB betting shop to back England to win the second Test match. Yes, you read that correctly. A small part of me was also hoping to bump into Tom Hunt so to ask him "what's the time?" and then wait in awesome anticipation at his answer. There was method to my madness. If England were fortunate enough to win the toss, bat first and pile on 400 then they would be favourites. Certainly it was not the 8-1 chance that the establishment was offering. The sharp-minded among you may point out that this was the same bookmaker who offered 200-1 about a dead horse winning a race and that although England's cricketers were at least alive, many only looked fit for the knacker's yard. Both were good points but I ignored them. I came over all righteous, stirring myself with a speech of Churchillian proportions. "If there is to be a miracle anywhere it will be here, stiffen the sinews for this leap of faith my friend and remember that with the Adelaide Oval overlooked by St Peter's Cathedral, this is the perfect venue for divine intervention. God is an Englishman". Nostrils flared and with pride in my heart I slapped £20 down and declared: "On England please!"

The cashier, with a look on her face as if I had just told her I was the second coming replied: "You want to bet on *England*?"

"Is the Pope Catholic?" I said.

With a wager out of the way the next task was to find my accommodation, which was in the district of Pooraka. I didn't know where Pooraka was. Nor, in fact, did the three-strong staff at the tourist office, who gathered in an excitable huddle to try to form some sort of consensus. They decided to scan their map and there was a collective Eureka! moment when one young lady planted her index finger and said: "Here it is... up near Para Hills." A concerned murmur followed. I knew what this grumble referred to. Para Hills was a district in north Adelaide which a guidebook warned was infamous for youngsters throwing rocks at buses. "Will you be okay?" asked the young lady. I thought I would be fine. A few kids throwing stones at buses was nothing and it was extraordinary to think such a 'danger' made it into a travel guide.

"Yep, I'll watch out for hoodlums lobbing pebbles while I'm hurtling along at 50mph in a ten-ton bus," I exclaimed. Of course finding Pooraka on the map was one thing, telling me how to get there was an altogether different challenge and the huddle reformed until I was directed to King William Street, which ran through the heart of the city from north to south.

King William Street was rather an odd sight because it was so ruddy big, looking out of sorts from the small town surrounds. Reputed to be the widest street of all of the Australian state capital cities, one had to be alert to cover the 130 feet and six lanes to get safely to the other side. It is flanked by striking office buildings and for a moment, you could be forgiven for thinking you were in a much bigger city than one which has a population, in its centre, of just 20,000. In that sentence you have Adelaide's charm. Adelaide and all its districts is actually home to more than one million yet the centre – organised in grid style with six roads, shown the way by the bold and brash King William, heading south and intersected by four others east to west – is kept cosy because it is entirely surrounded by parkland, acting like a moat to keep the sprawl of the suburbs from encroaching. The queue for the bus therefore was a long one.

The wait was a couple of minutes (always worth mentioning if not to put to shame the scandalous, death-inducing lingering done for London buses) and everyone on board was cheery, not looking in the least bit concerned about some oik emerging from the side of the road to hurl a lump of granite. I double checked with the driver that the bus would indeed drop me at Pooraka.

"Phew mate! Er, Pooraka eh? I think so."

This was not a good sign. I didn't understand why he said that he *thought* the bus would go to Pooraka. One would hope that at the very least the driver would *know* where he was going. Or was it that Pooraka was so nondescript and deserted that no-one had got off there before so he really didn't know where it was?

"Perhaps you'd be good enough to give me a shout when I need to get off?" I suggested in a clipped Home Counties tone, which made us both feel uncomfortable.

There was a pause before he turned to look at the road with a smile and said: "No worries, mate."

The bus made its way out the city, crossing the River Torrens into north Adelaide through the green zone and into dreary and dilapidated suburbs. The six-lane road would best be described as a motorway were it not for the shops alongside and families going about their business. We passed through communities with houses just like you see in *Neighbours*, then the out-of-town superstores. Slowly Adelaide disappeared before my eyes. Buildings became a rare sight. So too did a fellow passenger. Surely the driver had not forgotten Pooraka? We were picking up speed and to my darting eyes, were heading for desert. I looked at my watch. I had been travelling for 30 minutes.

I was in that awkward position of either asking the driver again and running the risk of making myself look a fool or sitting tight, hoping he hadn't forgotten, but if he had coming across as an even bigger Charlie. It was a familiar feeling. I had done the same in Amsterdam on a tram. The minutes ticked by, one by one the passengers departed and by the time I had plucked up the courage to ask the driver whether I had missed the stop, he just shrugged his shoulders and pointed to the sidings that we were about to roll into. At the speed we were travelling, however, I would soon be back in Brisbane so the driver would have to be tackled.

"Aw, sorry mate, I completely forgot," he said. "You'll have to walk twenty minutes back down the road there." I'm sure he had done this on purpose. Just because I was a Pom. The bus veered away leaving behind a puff of dust, which when it cleared revealed that I was in a no-man's-land. In the distance, and I really had to squint, I could just about make out a collection of buildings, which I assumed to be the oracular Pooraka. On went the backpack, which was just beginning to bite into the shoulders with that ripe and decisive pain which suggests a blister is imminent, and off I went walking back to whence I came. I took care with each step to check that I was not disturbing any Redbacks but that was easier said than done because of the weight on my back and the buffeting wind caused by the force of the trucks which bellowed past. Just as I raised a leg to carefully place down in the roadside undergrowth another juggernaut would shudder by. I was wobbling all over the place. Passing motorists looked at me and thought 'that drunkard will get himself killed'. There was a feeling of triumph when I saw the sign for the Pavlos motel yet that quickly dissipated when I noticed that what surrounded it was an unholy dump. This was not surprising given that the tourist office and bus driver did not know where the place was and, of course, that it was called Pooraka. Not the most charismatic of names. Reverse it and you get AKA Poor. It was just a small collection of buildings by a road big enough to be an interstate – although technically the next state, Northern Territory, was about a billion miles away – and two of them were motels, the Pavlos and the Pooraka Motor Inn. Both looked as awful as each other, the sort of motels that a drug addict would book to overdose in. I cursed my foolishness for ending up miles from the city and, it seemed, civilisation. In mitigation, in Brisbane rumours of Adelaide city centre hotels being fully booked spread like glandular fever at a school disco. After phoning a couple of hostels which I was told were full, I panicked. I'm not ashamed to admit it. So when I was told of a vacancy at the Pavlos, I took it. I entered the lobby and heard on the radio: "The war veteran who has been told he must die soon if he is to be buried in his local cemetery…" This was a backwater all right. The white-haired proprietor had a wild look in his eye as if he had not seen anyone for months. And why would he? The Pavlos Motel was a dump; he showed me to my room which had a lock which may as well have been made of Lego, there was no glass in the window, a wire mesh behind some flimsy plastic and the fridge (of course I needed one. I had to keep fresh the rack of lamb I had brought with me didn't I?) gurgled disconcertingly, giving off a burning smell. If I was not murdered in my bed by robbers who had cajoled a five-year-old in to forcing the door or simply flipped open the window, then I would be dead from carbon monoxide poisoning from an odious fridge. And was that a Redback in the corner? I clasped the owner's hand.

"Thanks for everything," I whimpered. "It was lovely knowing you."

Still with that look in his eye, he nodded and made a hasty exit. I clenched my fist, raised it to the heavens and shook it at those pesky Quaker and Puritan forefathers.

There was nothing else for it, for my own sanity I had to get out of there for the evening. At the very least a trip back into Adelaide was necessary because I had to eat.

Dining in Adelaide's 'eating out' area, which was Rundle Street, was a very pleasant experience. People laughed and joked outside the roadside cafes while boy racers in souped-up sports cars roared by as if cocking a snook at those bloody Puritans. I chose a Greek restaurant, if not so much for the food but to joke with the waitress that it was "all Greek to me" when she asked what I wanted from a confusing menu. I think she thought my hobby was to throw rocks at passing vehicles. On the walk to King William Street to catch my bus back to AKA Poor, I noticed some paving stones had one dollar coins glued into them. I found one worth about $90, which was the cost of a night at the Pavlos. That night I rested my head and dreamt about whether the Adelaide streets would be genuinely paved with gold.

I was up early for the first day of the second Test at the Adelaide Oval. Too early in fact. I had forgotten to factor in the time difference between South Australia and Queensland so with a couple of hours to go before play began, I was able to pick my spot on a grass bank and spreadeagle myself in distasteful fashion. Still, there was excitement in the air, particularly when Mike Gatting appeared holding an English flag just before the toss. As we all know, anything that Gatting holds in his hands he usually eats so it was the first surprise of the day to see that he did not try to scoff it down his gob. The second was that England won the toss and batted. The third was that the play was excruciatingly boring. To pass the time I was reduced to attempting amateur social anthropology.

There are a lot of people who will try to convince you that the Australians and English are one and the same by virtue of the latter ridding itself of undesirables on convict ships in the late 1700s. More than 300 years have made us somewhat different, however. For different, read superior (apart from, irritatingly, when it comes to sport). Take soap operas. *Neighbours'* old bag Helen Daniels was one of the world's oldest women before she finally put viewers out of their misery by dying in her sleep.

Lame. If she'd have been in *Eastenders*, she would have got struck by a JCB trying to save a baby from its path, made a remarkable recovery in hospital only to contract MRSA and then peg out. Art is another. We've had Turner, Constable, Gainsborough etc. Australia's contribution? Rolf Harris. 'Ahoo! Ahaah! Can you see what it is yet?' Yes Rolf … it's crap. This book could be filled with such examples.

The pursuit of watching cricket is no different in terms of exposing the gulf between cultures, both by the people who do it and the surrounds which they do it in. The interesting thing about Australian cricket fans is that for all their huff and puff about being in love with the game, when they actually attend a match they don't even watch the action. The English never take their eyes off it. Some, admittedly ones with a speech impediment, ill-fitting tank top and snot congealing around the nostrils, keep scorebooks with different coloured pencils for run denominations, two stop watches to register the precise length of time each batsman has batted and have an unnerving habit of turning to you and spouting unusual, nay useless, facts. 'That was his 178th run in the Championship … at home … on a Wednesday … wearing a cap.'

Australians will do anything but watch. Their first trick is to start making calls on a mobile phone to mates on the other side of the ground and when they answer they stand up, wave their arms and shout 'I'm here! I'm here!' For the next ten minutes you have to put up with a convoluted conversation as the two try to work out where each other is. 'Is that you? Are you wearing a hat? To the left of the scoreboard or the right?' Why don't they just agree to meet at a certain point in the lunch break? Why don't they sit down to stop obscuring the view of the person behind? Why don't they just try to watch the bloody game? It seems to me the only purpose this circus serves is so that the 'mates' don't actually bump into each other at all. Perhaps they find each other as irritating as everyone else does in the crowd.

Once that charade is out of the way conversation among our

Aussie pals' fellow spectators will soon turn to what t-shirts they are wearing. Now Aussies love to come to the cricket in a group and have a garment to mark the occasion. It usually says the name of the Test venue on it and the date, absolutely must have some green and gold with either a kangaroo, possum, koala, emu or cricketer. You get bonus points for all five. And on the back of the shirt, in big capital letters between the shoulder blades, must be the nickname of the person wearing it. Dooley, Stumps, Scottsy, Jezza, Marto, The Tank, Clipper, Strawbs, Burgerman, Twat, Thrush. And if they are not wearing a t-shirt with their name on, it is one which pays homage to beer. Bad Liver Must Be Punished, Beer Delivery Guy, I'm The Designated Passenger, No Such Thing As A Bad Beer... Just A Bad Attitude are some of the more popular. Hilarious.

The rest of the day will be spent yakking. They will chatter about anything apart from the cricket. Their conversation topics are beer, sheilas, Bradman, beer, sun cream, the sun, beer, Poms, pizza and beer. There is particular excitement if a woman wearing a t-shirt (with her nickname on, something like Juicy or Baps), brings back beer and pizza for her pals. 'Aw, that's what I call a sheila,' they'll shout before adding 'get yer kit off!'

At least it stops them singing. A rendition of 'I'd rather be a poofter than a Pom' was being sung by a group of five or six blokes all wearing custom-made t-shirts with the words 'Aussie Benders' on them. Only very occasionally, sandwiched between the staple cry of "Aussie, Aussie, Aussie" and "1-0, 1-0" did they come up with something original like "Warney fathered all you children, 'cos your wife wasn't satisfied," to the tune of Glory, Glory, Hallelujah.

None of this would happen at cricket matches in England, mainly because the people who go to watch are very, very old. They sit in deckchairs all day and do not make a sound. Not a peep. Often this is because they have died during play. But is there a commotion if an old timer is discovered to have passed on to the great pavilion in the sky? Nope. No-one mentions it, save for a reflective tut that the outgoing cricket fan has just missed out on so-and-so's second first-class fifty ... against the same opposition ... in August ... when rain curtailed play for 30 minutes in the morning ... and he had trifle for lunch.

You could say the Achilles heel of my argument is the Barmy Army. But, really, they don't make a great deal of noise, either, at least not until the effects of the alcohol kicks in around the tea break. Up until then they are quite content just to stand, slurp, sway, belch and sweat in the sun. Their ear-splitting tendencies do upset the Australians, largely because they think it is their right to be the ones behaving in a brash way. For the Test matches in Brisbane and Adelaide, the Barmy Army's official trumpeter, Bill Cooper, was banned from sounding his clarion call. It was proof, if ever we needed it, that in this world you've got to blow your own trumpet because sure as hell no one is going to purse their lips and blow it for you. The official reason given by Cricket Australia, who imposed the ban, was that it could be "used as a weapon" although I supposed that it depended where you stuck it.

The stadiums of course differ hugely in Australia compared to England. Picturesque Adelaide and Sydney aside, they are considered concrete carbuncles with little charm. I was not too fussed about that but regrettably this garishness translated itself to the cricket shops which could be found on site. Anyone who has ever been to a professional cricket match will attest that just in case the on-field play is stupefying, a classy, quirky, quintessential store selling meaningless tat is worth hours of fun. In Australia, grounds only sell baseball caps with the logo of the state side on and, come on reader you should know this one ... t-shirts. In England you can go to Worcester's New Road ground and buy a ruler which says 'I make it a rule to watch Worcester'. New lines being rushed out are a pencil case with the slogan 'you don't have to be a case to watch Worcester' and a thimble proclaiming 'you don't have to be a prick to watch Worcester'.

Immediately after day one I extricated myself from the Pavlos.

Never before had I considered that I might be happy at the prospect of sharing a room with seven other men – and in a room almost half the size of the one I frequented in Brisbane. The Shakespeare Backpackers Hostel in Waymouth Street was my new accommodation. The name was befitting of its clientele in that the majority were English, although that was where the similarity ended because most couldn't string a sentence together. Evidence of such in my room came in the form of two Chinese students, three barrow boys from Essex whose murder of the English tongue was something to behold, a Scouser and one familiar face.

"A-right mate, nice to meet yaw."

"What do you mean 'nice to meet you' Wayne, we roomed together in Brisbane? You kept me awake all night with your snoring."

"Him'sda geezer," laughed the Essex boys, John, Evan and Skillsy (I never found out his real name) in unison.

"Not me." he said.

Yet even the sight of Wayne did not sap the spirit. In fact, Wayne, myself, the Essex boys and the Scouser Shaun would prove to be inseparable for the next few days. Wayne was the glue which held fast the group insofar as the rest of us bonded by seeing who could best mimic his Norfolk accent.

The Essex boys had him down perfectly, although granted they would spend most of their time riling the oaf over his boasts of his success with the local women. It would begin with Evan suggesting he had charmed a local at the bar the previous evening. "That's nuffin mate," responded an irked Wayne. "I reckon they were all hedgepigs. I was getting a pizza (substitute another fast food stuff for another night) and the bird darn there gave me extra tawpings." At which point the boys, who all looked identical with their hair plastered in styling gel, cotton shirts and white trainers would burst into laughter. "Hedgepigs!" one would squeal. "Tawpings!" another.

While such hilarity was underway, I would talk to Shaun. He

had a slightly unnerving habit of appearing as though he was constantly looking for an opportunity to steal. A depressing stereotype, I know, but before you all start accusing me of 'racism', my mother was born in Liverpool, wet herself in the Cavern Club when the Beatles played live and can hotwire a car in 30 seconds flat.

Shaun had a pointy nose and a receding hairline that formed a V – pointing directly to his shifting eyes. He was compelling company, although I never relaxed because one couldn't be sure if he was telling the truth. Like the story about the footballer he knew.

"He was a real scally this lad," he said. "I mean proper naughty. He loved thieving. His club sent him down to play on-loan for some poxy lower league team and the lads there found out about his reputation so decided to set him up.

"The club captain was moving house and these lads had to help him. They said to my mate 'we're doing a job tomorrow, nice plush house, loads of stuff, you in?' He never needed a second invite.

"The players put one of the club shirts with my mate's name on the back in the wardrobe and when he turned up they said 'job's off, he's a fan of yours'. This bloke went upstairs, put on the shirt and came down and started unplugging the stereo. 'Always better to be robbed by a pal – come on, boys, look lively.'"

There was a ritual to our days. Go to the cricket, visit the Sky City casino because it offered free hot dogs, or 'snags' as they were known, and beer. It was a clever ruse because anyone taking the casino up on the offer would enter at the back of the building but could leave only via the front, meaning they had to walk through the casino. They must have made a fortune from sozzled Englishmen stumbling between the tables reckoning 'I'll just have one bet'.

I did not dabble. I didn't need to. The free food and drink was enticement enough and besides, I had backed Ricky Ponting to score most runs for Australia in the first innings, a wager that netted me £90. I had reinvested a fiver in Australia at 10-1, not because I thought they'd win, more for the souvenir of the slip as it was not often one would see them at such big odds.

Resisting temptation one evening in the casino I spotted commentator and former West Indies fast bowler Michael Holding at the roulette table. He was spraying his chips all over the place. He had never been so wayward as a bowler.

"You're spraying your chips all over the place," I mumbled. He heard me. I feared a rebuke but instead he let out a deep laugh and in that unmistakable Jamaica twang said: "You gotta improve your chances … it's only a warm-up for Melbourne."

"Ah, the Crown casino," I replied. "I'll see you in there."

"Doubt in, mon. Biggest in the world. Don't get lost now."

Of course when I returned to the hostel, buoyed by my gambling banter with the great man, I immediately told my roommates of my meeting.

Up piped Wayne. "That's nuffin mate…"

Wayne had begun to grate again. He was in particularly irritating form later that evening, the night before the last day of the Test match, when he threw his toys into the pub corner at discovering he had lost his expensive-looking phone. He got drunk, was generally obnoxious, disappeared and was found in his bunk later on, singing Barmy Army songs in his sleep.

Shaun, who had kept his counsel on our friend from Norfolk, nudged me and said "he's not all bad". I was almost incredulous until Shaun produced Wayne's phone from his pocket. "Do you need to call your mam?" he continued before giving me a wink with those shifty eyes. "Always better to be robbed by a pal."

Next morning, Shaun had packed his bags and left, never to be seen or heard from again. Well, by us at least. Wayne remained in an inconsolable state and I suppose if I had wanted to increase it I could have told him all about Shaun the Scouser and his late-night calls to his 'mam' on Merseyside. I kept quiet.

Besides, there was more misery on its way for the poor lamb. That day England managed to lose the Test from an almost impregnable position. It was quite something, although oddly inevitable. The air around the Oval in the morning had been thick with anxiety. By afternoon, as England slid towards ignominy, it was pure panic. It was all too much for one Barmy Army member. Barechested and with a Blackburn Rovers tattoo above his heart, he regurgitated his beer on to my feet, protected only by flip-flops. Bewildered, he reacted in the only way that such species can – to start singing. Such a sight makes it far easier to come to terms with the twinge of betrayal you get when taking pleasure from watching your country humiliated on the field of play in a foreign land.

It was only a momentary spasm of guilt, however. It was soon replaced by a tremendous feeling of pride that, thanks to Mr Ponting and Australia's remarkable win, I had defeated those pesky Puritans. To celebrate, I revisited the tourist office to see if there was a homage to the city's founders. "Can you tell me where I can find out about the Puritans?" I asked. The woman looked confused. "Are they a rock band?" she said.

Distance travelled: 18,635km
Won: £504
Lost: £194
Profit/loss: +£310
Target: £1,300

To be settled
£1 buy M Hussey series runs at 362
£125 England to win a Test 10-11
£70 S Warne top Australia wicket-taker evens
£1 sell J Langer series runs at 402

Chapter 6
Perth

An epic journey would not be complete without a period of contemplation. Well, that was my excuse to bugger around for a few days anyway. Perth, Western Australia was the perfect destination to sit down and have a good hard think about how far I'd come and where I would be going (we're talking metaphorically here, I had actually travelled 20,749km and would do a further 5,515 to Melbourne and Sydney before heading home). What I meant was: how was my financial situation and what could I do to make my target of £1,300 given I had only two cities to go and was nearly £1,000 behind where I should have been?

No matter. Calm and careful planning would be the way ahead. And as I said, Perth could not have been more ideal. It is the most isolated city on the planet, something which would lend itself to considered thought. Perfect isolation if you like. I would be living in luxury, relative to sharing shoeboxes with snoring, solecistic, stealing scamps. I would stay with Jon and Lizzie, two friends from London who had emigrated, in their flat in a converted biscuit factory with views of the sea in Fremantle, or Freo as the locals called it.

Jon, an engineer, was working in Perth and before embarking on his profession, worked in a bookmakers in Swiss Cottage.

"Was better paid than my first engineering job," he reminded me. "Because one punter who would win big regularly would give me tips."

Alas, this was not how we met. That was through Lizzie, who had been childhood friends with Flatmate's sister. She was busy shaping Australia's future by teaching in a Freo school. It promised to be a good one, the future that is. From my early travels it had struck me how unfortunate those of us were who did not have pilfering ancestors. Had my great, great granddad been more shifty, I too could have grown up in Australia, enjoying the no worries culture, endemic of the beautiful weather and an outdoor life which the open space demanded one live.

Freo was one of the best examples. It was the most relaxed of the places I had visited. A haunt for writers, musicians and thespians, it was the equivalent of London's Camden Town, but without the dirt, stink and students. Its arty ambience was nicely juxtapositioned by the masculine grunt of the working port, which made the cappuccino strip all the more enjoyable because sipping a latte is more pleasant when people in earshot are doing back-breaking work.

During one such lazy afternoon with a coffee I picked up the local newspaper and spied a story which stirred me, a reminder that despite Australia's laid-back reputation there were still occasions when the country would sit bolt upright. Before leaving Adelaide, I visited the Migration Museum, which was housed in the city's old Destitute Asylum for the poor and homeless. Apt considering if all went wrong on the expedition I would be at least one of those.

Now you may know that down under immigration has been a bit of a hot topic to say the least; they do have a museum dedicated to it after all. I'm not saying all Australians are racist, that would be a sweeping generalisation, but it is difficult not to think so when, in both the first two Test matches, the home faithful sang "I'd rather be a Paki than a Pom". And no-one batted an eyelid in Brisbane when Andrew Symonds, who is black, came to the wicket and a green and gold clad fan shouted "have a go you wog!"

The Migration Museum made for a fascinating hour or so

to learn how the White Australia Policy (or rather a collection of policies and bills which ceased in 1973) would allow any immigrant in, providing they could pass a written examination (in Swedish) and the important role migrants had in making Australia the country it was. At the end of the tour, the museum asks the question 'should we let them stay?' with regard to a heartbreaking tale of a family from Papua, who had recently fled from Indonesian brutality. They were playing devil's advocate, of course, expecting their visitors to reply in the affirmative after having their eyes opened by the museum's display and literature. The visitors who replied, using the Post-it notes provided, with "yes, but only if they don't form ghettos" and "no bloody way, send them all home" were just trying to be controversial. Weren't they? The best came from a schoolkid, however, who wrote "they can stay at my house, my mum's a good cook".

So on page 29 of *The Gazette* we had a story headlined 'Filipino Fits Right In' which told how a Filipino (surprise, surprise) was "helping fill the skills gap" by working in the shipyard. It seemed a ludicrous story in terms of actual 'news' and seemed to be saying 'see, they're not all bad' especially when his boss was quoted as saying "he sounds more like an Aussie every day". Next to the story was a nomination form for a people's award in Western Australia. I took a couple of minutes to fill it in in honour of our shipyard friend, scribbling "helping fill the skills gap and sounding more like an Aussie every day" under the section 'reason for nomination'.

At this point you may be wary that I was, in fact, being just lazy, shunning contemplation and mental stocktaking for getting coffee highs and confusing the organisers of community awards. That would be to misunderstand that one cannot think clearly without being fully relaxed. It was a work in progress.

If I wasn't pontificating about snippets in the local rag, I would wander around the flat in my pants – never underestimate the power of such a pastime to help one chill out – or chortle at the sign outside a nearby body-piercing parlour: 'we make holes in ya skin, not ya wallet'.

I also took a keen interest in why Western Australians seemed to have an obsession with acronyms. They loved them. Every association, organisation, or group had to have WA plonked in front of it. For example, if you needed the fire brigade because your house was burning down you would call the WAFS (Fire Service), if you needed to find a bed and breakfast in the aftermath get on the phone to the WABBA (Bed and Breakfast Association), when you're ready to rebuild your home don't fall foul of a WAPCA (Planning Commission Act), otherwise you'll never be able to get the work done by the WAMBA (Master Builder Association).

Naturally, I was salivating at the prospect of some poor, naïve group not realising that their WA acronym spelt something filthy, and hence incredibly amusing. So I would scour the business directory, hoping to discover that the National Crime Authority had an office in WA. The best giggle I could manage was WACY – Western Australian Citizen of the Year. I was beginning to fret that I would never be satisfied until I chanced upon a leaflet advertising local events. And there it was. The Western Australia Naturists' Club had a meeting scheduled. I absolutely had to attend. It was such a release that in my rush to share with the world that I was going out for a WANC, I locked myself out. It proved to be, if you'll excuse me, a masterstroke.

I thought that I could spend another afternoon on Cappuccino Strip to pass the time until Lizzie and Jon returned. I had not reckoned on being attacked by a magpie every time I tried to leave the surrounds of the biscuit factory. Flailing arms and panicked shouts of "fuck off! fuck off!" did not deter my swooping and squawking assailant. In fact it seemed genuinely up for a fight. Round one went to the magpie when I lost my balance trying to swat it away, crumpling in a heap on the road with each of my flip-flops jettisoned, pointing in different directions as markers to the chaos which had unfolded. I ran away very fast indeed for a man without anything on his feet. Rounds two and three also went to the magpie as I attempted to salvage my footwear. But not round four. Oh no. Picking up the biggest stick I could find I was quite prepared to beat the magpie to death if I had to. Luckily for him he spotted the weapon and decided not to attack. The stick is mightier than the sword my feathered fiend, although it must be said that when I was told I would be "fighting off birds with a stick down under" that was not what I had in mind.

With my flip-flops safely retrieved, I sat on the porch and waited. Boy, did I get some good, hard thinking done for the next couple of hours. I resolved to close my two spread bets on Mike Hussey and Justin Langer runs respectively. It is a spread betting rule that one should only ever close a trade when one has a very good reason. Mine was that I needed the money to get to Melbourne. Hussey netted £127 and Langer cost me £25.50.

Spirits were high. Lizzie and Jon had become something of a surrogate mum and dad. On their arrival back from work I would make them a cup of tea and ask them about their day. On the weekend they took me to the beach, although I was not allowed to go into the water because a recent Great White shark attack had left one poor chap minus a leg. They also invited me to a picnic with their friend Jayne, who said she knew the victim and without a trace of mischief announced that he was a "stand up guy". The mind had never felt fitter for a wager on the third Test at the WACA (Western Australia Cricket Association to you and me).

They say talk is cheap but in the case of the famous Channel Nine commentary team it can be very expensive. Without a ticket for the first day at the WACA all I thought I needed to watch the action was a sofa and a television set. It only took 10 minutes to realise a pair of ear muffs would have been useful, too.

Ian Chappell, Ian Healy and Bill Lawry wasted little time in rubbishing England's new-ball assault. Fair dinkum Aussies the world over were at risk of taking the rantings of their former heroes to the heart of their wallet by buying Australia's first innings runs at 450 on the spreads. Chappell wanted a "minimum of four slips, maybe five", Healy was convinced England had no answer to the hosts' fast start while Lawry, no doubt wiping away tears of joy with the Australian flag, just screamed "shot!" every delivery, even if the ball squirted off the edge.

Despite England chipping away at Australia's batting order, the bias band, with Lawry taking the role as jeerleader-in-chief, had the same effect on my subconscious – so much for the clarity. It was almost hypnotic. Even frenzied attempts to ram cotton buds down my lugholes whilst humming loudly could not prevent the spell taking hold and I bought Australia's runs at 351. Fortunately Andrew Symonds' withering 6-6-4 assault on Monty Panesar sent Lawry's voice so high-pitched that only dogs could hear him. Momentarily I was able to recover my senses and close out the bet for a £98 profit.

Still feeling woozy, a walk on the beach was required. The Fremantle Doctor, Perth's famous wind, whipped sand into my legs at a rate which fooled me into thinking Lawry was trying a new form of witchcraft by sticking pins and needles into a Barmy Army rag doll.

The refreshing stroll was enough to release me from the hex. England took Australia's final wicket just as I took a seat on my couch. Lawry was probably having a lie down on his.

My surrogate parents were tremendously supportive of my quest. 'Mum' showed the same interest in my winning betting slips as a real mother would for a son's first unfathomable scribble with a crayon. Indeed for the duration of my visit the 'Australia to win second Test' slip was pinned to the fridge. 'Dad' was less forthcoming with praise, instead nodding sagely at the piece of paper every time he went to collect a beer. He was more hands on, suggesting I get "back on the horse" after a £26 loss on Andrew Strauss runs to buy Paul Collingwood's. Wise. The result was an £84 booster.

He was most instrumental, however, in what would be the biggest wager. When Ian Bell and Alastair Cook were still together in the fourth innings, with the score around 150 for one and England needing an impossible 557 to win, Australia were as big as 1-3 for victory. I thought it was a crazy price. So did 'Dad', who with relish started to work out that Australia needed to average a wicket every 15 overs and that throughout Test history, sides in the fourth innings averaged a wicket every 11 overs. It was some statistic. The argument that England were crap would have been enough for me but 'Dad's' maths gave extra confidence. £300 of my winnings went on Australia. England's runs were sold for £2 at 405, too. Almost immediately Bell was out and Collingwood went soon after. Australia won the next day and in doing so retained the Ashes. A nice little urner. The urn had turned etcetera.

Indeed it had. With two venues still to visit, I was only £522.50 from my target. That was wins of only £261.25 in Melbourne and Sydney respectively. For the first time, I thought I was going to pull it off.

'Mum' had felt rather left out when the two men of the house were dissecting gambling strategy, so before I left for Christmas in Melbourne, she would be appeased with a visit to the WATA (Western Australian Trotting Association). It is a fact that any woman who has been horseracing will tell you that they 'won loads' because they are 'some sort of psychic'. What they won't tell you is that they backed every horse that was running.

"But I won £10!"

"No you didn't. There were 10 horses. You had £3 on each of them so you lost."

"But the man gave me back £10, I can show it to you... look."

On arrival at the WATA, 'Mum' had to be taken aside and told not to get too carried away.

"Right," I said. "Let's watch the first race to see what we can learn, then we'll study the racecard, we'll only bet each-way and I believe, if memory serves, about 40 per cent of favourites win in harness racing so that gives us something to think about..."'Dad' nodded in agreement, impressed by this show of maturity. "What do you think?" I added, turning to 'Mum'. She was no longer in earshot, instead she could be seen in the distance waving a fistful of dollars in the face of the cashier.

At least she did not back all 11 runners, although she did fall into the hole that many female racegoers disappear, choosing their steed by virtue of "the colour of its fur", the colour of the jockey's "jumper" or which had the "kindest face" (horse or jock). The blue, red and white diagonal stripes of Demoralizer had caught 'Mum's' eye. If only she had paid attention to the massive clue in the name or, slightly ambitious this, the form comments in the racecard. "Demoralizer will need a miracle to win". It was clear that instead of wasting some of the big sums (I had a few throwaway fivers) of the last few days by wagering on something I knew nothing about, my efforts would be put to better use trying to keep 'Mum' from ruin.

It was a good move. I watched the first race and spotted nothing, apart from that harness racing was a bit like chariot racing – you know, *Ben-Hur* but without the thrill, death or camp costumes. The jockeys, or drivers as they are known, sit on a 'sulky' directly behind the horse's backside. Most unedifying is the position they find themselves in. They look a bit like someone who has had to rush to the toilet, surprised by the violent reaction of last night's jalfrezi with legs splayed out in front, their head retreating into their shoulders and arms forced forward for balance as the juddering and uncomfortable ride begins. If it was uncomfortable to compete in, watching it was likewise. Whichever horse got in front on the first bend was certain to win with the carriages' width and speed too great respectively for any overtaking.

It was left to 'Mum' to provide the entertainment with her shouts of encouragement for Demoralizer. They started in positive fashion with a hopeful "you can do it!" before becoming increasingly aggressive as the race unfolded. On the final bend she was reduced to screeching "Thrash it! Thrash it with the whip you fool!". This sentence has been censored for the extraordinary number of swear words she managed to cram in.

Demoralizer lived up to its name. Trudging back to the car, passing underneath the WATA sign, 'Mum' mumbled "WATA waste of money, more like."

Distance travelled: 20,749km
Won: £1,023
Lost: £245.50
Profit/loss: +£777.50
Target: £1,300

To be settled
£125 England to win a Test 10-11
£70 S Warne top Australia wicket-taker evens

Chapter 7

Melbourne

Dial M for misery, malady, murder. Take your pick. I just don't know what it is about places beginning with 'M'. Whenever I go to an 'M', or bet on a sport taking place at an 'M', I have a miserable time. Melbourne was no different. Previously in my punting life I had suffered terrible losses in Mohali, Mumbai, Middlesbrough and Manchester. Indeed, the mere mention of the name of the latter northern city makes me feel all peculiar.

As a youngster travelling to Old Trafford with Dad, the real one not the Perth replacement, to watch our Gloucestershire no hopers take on the mighty Lancashire in a one-day cricket semi-final, I was struck down with a headache, vomited all over the car dashboard and then broke down in tears when Dad, typically for the male race, phoned up Mum asking what he should do. And she said 'bring him home'.

About 20 years later I would return to Manchester for a Test match between England and Pakistan. I lost £200 one day on a buy of Pakistan runs. A few days later I lost £200 on the same bet. To cap it all, I missed a promised night out with the sponsor's dolly birds because I had eaten something dodgy and was crapping through a button hole.

My experience in Melbourne put it on a par with Manchester. To make the most of the misery I suffered, I have reproduced my diary, word for word, of this particular spell of my journey. It is not for the faint-hearted.

Wednesday, December 20

Adam Gilchrist and chronic knee-injury victim Michael Vaughan are on flight from Perth to Melbourne. Saw their bags come off before everyone else's. While watching Vaughan's bags go round spot that the luggage handlers had fun at his expense by putting health and safety sticker on each one warning: "Heavy. Bend knees when lifting."

The rest of us wait for 30 minutes, perfect people watching time. Some stand patiently and watch every item like a predator eyeing its prey as it moves slowly past, others bob and weave through crowd with glaring eyes and nose in the air, sniffing out their brand of leather holdall. This does not make stuff arrive quicker.

The rest chatter inanely. Most of them women, who treat it as some sort of coffee morning. "Ooh, it's just like the *Generation Game*, isn't it?" No. Suitcase, suitcase, suitcase, rucksack, suitcase, suitcase...

Accommodation is £15 a night Victoria Hall. Décor and clientele seem to be inspired by the building opposite – Melbourne Gaol, where Aussie hero Ned Kelly was hung. My single room (treating myself for Christmas) has horrible smell of socks. Plethora of stains on grey carpet do not bear thinking about.

Fellow guests appear to be mostly drug addicts. In discussion with hollow-eyed rake-like bloke, he suddenly passes out and lands in heap on floor. Run away quickly back to room.

Thursday, December 21

Some fellow more profound than you or I once said talent was hitting a target no-one else could hit and genius was hitting a target no-one else could see. How he would describe Shane Warne, who announced his retirement today to a stunned country, may have even troubled his intellect.

There was a warning that the leg spinner was a bowler of a super ability when he spun his first Ashes delivery past a beleaguered Mike Gatting. Warne would not even have been able to see any of his three targets, least of all the off bail that was dislodged, thanks to Gatt's considerable gut. As many a joker has said since, "it would never have got past him had it been a cheese roll."

The real mark of the man is his wickets tally. Warne should claim his 700th Test victim at the MCG, his home ground, in the Boxing Day Test. Ian Healy, who used to keep wicket to Warne, admits on television that he, along with other cricket greats, thought no-one would ever reach such a goal. Warne disagreed. And you know what that means. I could do with a bit more of his genius coming to the fore for my top Australia series wicket-taker bet.

Friday, December 22

Melbourne is a big city. Something of a culture shock after Brisbane, Adelaide and Perth – reminiscent of average-sized English towns.

You can, though, get from one end to the other on foot in 30 minutes, a blessing with the purse strings tightening. Melbourne in festive mood. A 'Chrissy Countdown' clock in a department store is wowing the locals. Think of friends and family back home and smile at cash I'm saving on presents. Back in cell, sorry room, take my mind off smell of socks by drawing a cartoon of two snowmen, with huge pieces of coal for eyes. "Dark in here isn't it?" says one to the other. "Who said that?"

Saturday, December 23

Visit Melbourne Aquarium. Highlight is not the sting rays or even sharks. Nope. It is the book in shop warning that symptoms of a shark attack are "severed limbs". In what will hopefully not be connected, decide to sell former friend Mike Hussey's match runs at 90 for £2. He's made six consecutive scores of more than 50 and can't defy law of averages again.

Sunday, December 24

Never bet drunk is gambling's oldest adage. Pity I ignore it stumbling in to Crown Casino on Christmas Eve after festive fizz. This is biggest casino in southern hemisphere. It is responsible for 17% of all Victoria's tax income. Two kilometres from one side to the other so bearings are immediately lost. So too is £100 at Blackjack. Doubling one's stake after each losing hand is unwise. Incredible, unfathomable loss of discipline. I can't spot Michael Holding, either.

Monday, December 25

Christmas Day. Still in casino. Can't find way out. Outside it is Melbourne's coldest day for 150 years. Total time spent trying to find exit reaches 12 hours. Oh, all right four of them were in the nightclub. Lack of coordination a strong theme. Total losses reach £175 thanks to a continuing reckless Blackjack strategy and not-reckless-enough Poker game plan. I must be ill or something. On cold, lonely walk to 'prison' I pass a bar which is playing John Lennon ditty "So this is Christmas… and what have you done?" Exactly.

Open Christmas gifts from 'Mum' and 'Dad'. A 500g Toblerone bar – you can always tell from the wrapping – and *First Field Guide to Australian Birds* book. 'Mum' highlights the text on Magpies which reads "if magpies defending nests become aggressive, wear a hat, or take another route". Disappointed no mention of beating to death with sticks.

Tuesday, December 26

A Victorian I met in Brisbane promised "chicks with their tits out" at the MCG on Boxing Day. The only tits on view are England and myself. I boob by failing to show guts to sell their runs at 325. Costly error. I see Warne claim his 700th Test wicket, though. Only 89,155 others can make such a boast. Beginning to come down with some sort of flu.

Wednesday, December 27

Rudyard Kipling advised we should treat triumph and disaster, those two impostors, the same. The problem with Kipling was that he never had a spread bet in his life, otherwise he would have kept his trap shut.

Had he made such ricks as selling Andrew Symonds' runs at 37 for £2 on the second day of the fourth Test, 'If' would never have been penned. He probably wouldn't have been able to afford the ink. Only scribbling I feel like doing when watching Symonds cruise to 154 at a cost of £234 is suicide note.

Every time Symonds finds the ropes the noose tightens – £8 for every four and £12 when he clears them. For each one the 80,000 crowd roars. Do they know about my bet and are taking perverse pleasure from my nightmare? Feels like it. Even a £168 win on the Hussey run sell cannot prevent darkness descending.

Losses are particularly galling because when God was handing out the brains, Symonds was in the nets. On one Australia away tour he was in a shopping mall and entered a prize draw to win a fancy car. "When's the draw made?" he asked. "The 31st," came the reply. "In that case I'll look forward to your call on the 32nd." Try to remember Kipling.

"Keep your head while all around are losing theirs." Fail. Buy England runs for £1.50 at 320.

Discover cause of awful smell in hostel room: my socks.

Thursday, December 28

A further £238.50 disappears quicker than England's batsmen as they are bowled out for 161. I'm down to a profit of a measly £298. More merry hell than Merry Christmas. Times hard. Betting funds critical. Ration Toblerone. Sell my digital camera for £50 to only other non-druggie in hostel. Sleep past breakfast and through to lunch to save meal money. Hunger pains do not hurt as much as the pain of losing money. Go to every supermarket in city to see if they're giving away any free food on sticks. A low point.

Saturday, December 29

A money-saving lie-in until noon and then to Melbourne Museum, which is not only free, but is also hosting the Ashes exhibition. Topical.

I learn that no-one knows what is inside the tiny little urn, making a mockery of the hoo-hah, in particular Matthew Hayden, who cried like a girl who had just had her bra strap pinged by Superman when Australia retained them. You don't even know what you're crying over you fool.

Theories abound what the terracotta urn contains. One is that a bail was burned following a friendly match between Ivo Bligh's England team on 1882 tour – the year after the famous obituary was penned – and members of the Rupertswood estate, home of Melbourne Cricket Club boss Sir William Clarke. Sir Willy's wife and her chums decided to burn a bail and present the Ashes in an urn to Bligh. Others say it was a lady's veil. Others say more bails were burned after the third Test between England and Australia. Whatever. A load of willy's and bails.

Everyone missing point. Burning of things – whatever they are – can be looked at two ways. Over-exuberance or vandalism. I would have slapped an ASBO on the lot of them.

Sunday, December 30

Eat last piece of Toblerone. Pleased with myself that it has lasted this long. Otherwise feeling increasingly unwell. Flu was replaced by gurgling stomach, loud enough at least to muffle odd grunting noises coming from next room along. Took stroll to Carlton Gardens. Was momentarily amused to hear Aussie moron pronounce façade "fuck-ade" when describing to his wife the Royal Exhibition Building. Then stomach lurched violently into action and a race against time ensued to get back to hostel. Lose. Carlton Gardens' array of pretty flowers made nose spring into action. Sneeze sparked loss of control of tightened bottom cheeks. As gingerly moved each leg forward, a single small ball of poo made its way down my right trouser leg and flew out the exit, rolling along the pathway towards Mrs Fuck-ade.

Distance travelled: 23,430km
Won: £1,191
Lost: £893
Profit/loss: +£298
Target: £1,300

To be settled
£125 England to win a Test 10-11
£70 S Warne top Australia wicket-taker evens

Chapter 8
Sydney

Here is a sentence you do not want to hear from your new host after a disastrous betting week. "I live just behind the casino." It came from the mouth of Baz, who I would stay with in Darling Harbour, as I made my way from the airport to his flat on New Year's Eve. Here is another sentence you do not want to hear from your new host after he has enquired about one's gambling. "Aw look, don't worry about that mate, we're gonna smash into it… I've got plans."

As I had feared. Baz was known for his excessive behaviour – his smoking and gambling was worth in tax to the New South Wales government what the Crown Casino was to Victoria – and would most likely respond to any quibble by myself that his "plans" would bankrupt me with "why are you English such poofs?" We were different, Baz and I. Reserved, retiring, rational, responsible. Baz was none of those things. His social network profile gave the best indication of the man.

Activities:
Philandering

Interests:
Food, Nurses, Inflatable Penises, Y-Fronts, Ciggies, VBs

Favourite Music:
Sex Funk Rock

Favourite Movies:
The Warne Supremacy, The Warne Identity

Favourite Books:
Wisden

It was no accident that Baz's activities and interests mirrored those of Shane Warne, who had famously been caught philandering with some blondes and an inflatable penis by a British tabloid newspaper. Baz revered the man. They even looked alike. Baz had the same chubby cheeks as his idol and there was more than a passing resemblance in build to Warne's days when he ate nothing but grilled cheese sandwiches.

Baz played his cricket in the spirit of his idol, too. In other words he was a mouthy so and so. During a quintessential English village cricket match a few years back, Baz, who was schooled in Berkshire close to where I grew up, misread the intensity. It was white picket fence stuff, a handful of spectators had just returned from church, their children were playing in the long grass after too much ginger beer and the sun was shining, ensuring any thirst for competitive action evaporated. Good old Blighty! But being an Aussie, Baz's spirit was not diluted. Oh no. He was to open the bowling and was fired up.

His first delivery was a wide to first slip and bounced three times. "Fack! Fack! You facking fack! Get yer shit together!" he screamed.

The locals had never heard language like it. One old lady choked on her scone and the vicar reopened the church for those seeking refuge.

But let's not do a disservice to the man. He was a 'good bloke' as the Aussies would say and despite Baz living up to the stereotypical image of his countrymen in his spare time, during business hours he was hugely successful. He ran his own computer business (vague I know but when anyone mentions such an industry I shut down) and it was doing well enough for him to afford a pad in Darling Harbour, an inlet to the south of the Sydney Harbour Bridge and home to bars, restaurants, the obligatory aquarium that every big city must have by law and, of course, the casino.

Darling Harbour was named after Ralph Darling, the governor of New South Wales for six years from 1825. To the people of New South Wales he was anything but a darling. His was a rule of tyranny. Under his orders prisoners were tortured and his apparent obsession with domination extended as far as preventing people from having a good time. He completely banned drama or theatre of any kind, arguing that the continual pickpocketing and burglary of the patrons in previous establishments was unacceptable (he was probably right, this was a colony after all). A theatre was not established until two years after Darling was summoned back to England – to much public rejoicing. Today, there are two theatres in his harbour alone. Both are in the casino, though, suggesting that luvvie-hater Darling might have had a point.

If Baz had said he lived behind the theatre I would not have been so worried as I knocked on his door. Living up to his billing, he opened it wearing his boxers, a vest and singing "Ch, Ch, Changes" by David Bowie.

After exchanging pleasantries and gifts – I gave him a poster from the *Melbourne Herald Sun* advertising the Boxing Day Test which had unfortunately been designed in a way so 'Test' jutted into 'Day', instead spelling 'Gay', he gave me a beer – we sat on his balcony and watched the famous New Year's Eve Sydney fireworks. If I strained my neck to within an inch of snapping it while hanging precariously over the railing, I could just about see the Harbour Bridge and as the first crackles and screams from the pyrotechnical show began, I vowed to forget about my gambling strife and ensure I made the most of my time with my chum. At that point I wouldn't even have minded if Baz had suggested going to the casino.

"Ordinarily mate I'd say we nip over the road and spend our future children's inheritance but we've got a party to go to ... have you got a jacket?"

"'Fraid not, didn't think there would be much call for it."

"No worries, this place we're going requires that garb, you can borrow one of mine."

As I mentioned earlier, Baz and I were very different people. We were also different in terms of size. I was built like a folded ironing board and Baz a couple of tumble driers stacked atop one another.

"You look great," he said as I disappeared underneath a particularly unpleasant beige number.

"I don't," I said. "I look like I'm on a night out celebrating the removal of my Siamese twin. I'll never pull in this."

"You haven't met many Aussie birds then?" laughed Baz.

You will forgive me that I can't remember the name of the establishment that we frequented that night on King Street. Early on I do recall, however, making myself repellant to every woman in the place when I attempted to remove the beige blanket. In flapping my arms and contorting my face when trying to extricate myself, I succeeded in convincing one poor girl that I was having an epileptic fit.

"He's doing a lot of bumping and jerking," she told Baz.

"Yeah but he'll only keep it up for a few minutes. Now me, I can go all night," he winked.

There is a large memory gap between that incident and how we came to be ejected. Suffice to say I do believe that Baz was unfortunate enough to stumble upon a nurse and after uttering a few misplaced sentences which included the words 'y-fronts' 'inflatable' and 'penis' we were escorted from the premises.

Something for the weekend, sir? A bit of slap and tickle? No thanks, just a pokie for me. Apologies for the innuendo-laced vernacular but I am talking about the poker slot machines found in Australian pubs and clubs which have a jackpot chance of one in 53 million (phwoaar!). They are the risqué, winking, showing a bit of leg minx that Aussies fell in love with in the 1950s and have remained faithful to ever since.

Eyes pop and tongues loll at the mere mention of the word down under and the charm of these machines does not discriminate: male or female, pauper or politician have come under their spell. It is understandable. Throughout history the human race has been enchanted by anything that is shiny, pretty or flashes its eyes in a come-to-bed manner. The pokie does just that with its easy nature, whirring music and twinkling lights.

Sadly, most who get involved with such a hussy ends up a broken individual; something I was reminded of on the first day of the new year. It didn't begin until 5pm when I awoke from my slumber on the floor of Baz's apartment and I turned on the television news in time to catch a sobering item regarding a Sydney woman's obsession with the pokies. Anne must have been in her sixties. She said: "I don't think they're fair dinkum at all" and "you almost become addicted to the losing" – soundbites which would have been black comedy had she not lost her home, savings and tried to kill herself.

The narrator said there were "thousands like her". To be exact, 300,000 across Australia and 100,000 of them in New South Wales. Legally introduced in the state in 1956, the addictive nature of these dollar-guzzling machines had been underestimated.

A bit of harmless fun, people thought. Immediately Aussies jumped into bed with them, fumbling around in wonderment like teenage boys coming to terms with the convolutions of the bra strap. Eventually they got the hang of things and fell in love, reckoning that first decent win was the start of things to come. Payouts could be relied upon, offering the sort of security which meant they felt like they wanted to take a pokie home and make cooing noises while stroking its buttons (I don't think I've taken this analogy too far by the way).

The outcome was somewhat different. Just like the promises made at the start of every relationship – 'of course we'll still have sex' and 'I won't mind if we watch the football instead of my favourite soap' – they were broken. Hearts too.

Pokies are essentially just like the slot machines one might find in the corner of a British pub, often standing idle because no-one really knows how they work. Australians learnt quickly to catastrophic consequences, personally and politically. The fateful day when pokies were legalised has left Australians with no way out from the misery.

There are addicts. Of course there are. But there is dependence on all forms of gambling. One cannot really exist without the other. I am not about to start claiming that because of their addictive nature pokies should be banned, condemning them as evil and that governments who legalised them are responsible for opening some sort of punting Pandora's box. It would be churlish of me to do that, making the thousands of words which have preceded this extract utter hypocrisy.

What I would argue is that pokies are a greater problem than they should be. Why? Because the politicians had been seduced, too. We'll take the New South Wales government as an example. They got greedy. To the extent that the NSW government allowed more than 110,000 poker machines in the Sydney area, making it the pokie capital of the world. Ten per cent of the world's total pokies, and more than half of the 200,000 pokies in Australia, can be found there. All of those machines account for about $1.5bn a year in taxes. But it is not really how many, but where they have been allowed which should cause consternation: pubs.

One of the effects of alcohol, as we all know, is a loss of judgement. From harmless incidents like Baz trying to improve his philandering skills to tragedies on the roads. A government would not allow a pub to run a car rental from behind the bar. So why should it actively encourage its people to booze and bet at the same time, a car crash of a combination? Eventually the results are the same, just a bit farther down the road.

Across Australia, state government has become reliant on the huge tax payouts, not to mention the donations they receive from the pubs and clubs. A thank you for the extra machines they have been allowed to install and increase in licensing hours.

It is not just pokies, it is the TAB bookmakers too. One can get a beer and have a bet, a bizarre experience for an Englishman, who would only be subconsciously aware that the two are a no-no. In the UK there is a law stating that a bookmaker cannot even be next door to a pub.

The cocktail of gambling and grog safeguarded Australia's place as the country with the world's biggest gambling problem. Official figures from Australian gambling statistics show that Australians lost $15.3 billion in 2002-3. Punters in NSW were the biggest losers with $6.3bn down the drain. Of that, $3bn was lost on pokies in clubs, and $1.4bn lost on pokies in pubs. Total state government tax revenue from gambling was more than $3.9bn (up by $150m from 2001-2).

As a gambler it is trying enough to see people wasting their money on pokies when their chance of a return is small. Make that infuriating, however, when punters are not given the protection they deserve from bad, bad choices.

What also confuses is why pokie players cannot see that their habit is so futile, so damaging. But here we are discussing the complexities of addiction. Never would I attempt to seriously pontificate or educate about why Tom is a compulsive gambler but Dick and Harry only like the occasional flutter. You need a degree for that.

What I do understand is the difference between the sort of betting that I do (sports bets which have logic and statistical research as the cornerstones) and those that the pokie maniac attempts. The aspirations are smaller for a start. I suppose what keeps the pokie player coming back is this fantasy figure, one with nice legs, a big chest and a winning smile. Me? I'm thinking about the more important things in life: can she cook? Can she clean? Not can she, er, ahem.

My kind of betting is attractive because it can do the lot. I know where I stand. My tea is on the table when I get home from work and it is ready with my pipe and slippers when I'm finished. I'm getting nostalgic, of course; this is what it's like when it's going well. When it isn't going well? It's horrible. And that is what stops me chasing what the pokie player chases. The perpetual misery, or as Anne said, "addiction to losing".

I found it hard to imagine standing at a pokie, feeding a dollar into the slot, pushing the button, waiting a few seconds for the machine to signal defeat – and then doing it again – hundreds of times.

The anatomy of such a wager compared to a football, racing, cricket or any other sports bet is fundamentally different. The man who stands in front of the pokie can only *hope* to be lucky enough to hear the clatter of coins. A sports bettor at least has an *expectation* of victory, at least he should have if he has done some research, and an array of emotions as the action unfolds. The anatomy of such a losing bet is infinitely more interesting. I reckon one goes through five emotional stages. Starting with the one which probably means I keep coming back for more – expectation.

When I hand over my money I am convinced that my judgement will be proved correct because I have done a wealth of research. If I am asked why I have placed my money on so and so, there will almost be a snort of derision aimed at the inquisitor. The sort of snort chums of General Custer would have heard when they asked him "are you sure we don't need reinforcements?" It is quickly followed by fear. More specifically the fear of being wrong. Yes, bettors are nothing if not a fickle bunch. What will trigger it? Oh, anything. Perhaps memories of past misplaced cockiness, the flick of a horse's mane, the strut of an opposition player.

Once the bet is underway this feeling is replaced by expectation again. Then fear. Back to expectation. Flip-flopping between the two in line with the ebb and flow of the contest until it is clear that fear has won out and expectation, beaten and bruised, can only emerge if there is a miracle.

Stage three is the worst. I panic; at how much money is lost or, if it is a spread bet, how much could be lost. Mentally I attempt the mathematics and with each equation the dread tightens its grip around my throat as I begin to realise the sum of my fears. The heart more than skips a beat, it yo-yos up and down, clanging into the rib cage to send vibrations through the body. This will only subside when more mental arithmetic is attempted, adding up all the possessions which could be sold. "I might get 25 quid for the stereo, that TV can go … do I really need a bed?"

Anger is next. This will be directed at myself and inanimate objects or, indirectly, at other people. This anger can reach dangerous levels if I'm unfortunate enough to be at the sporting event, in which case thousands of people happily enjoying their day, cheering on their team (as they are quite entitled to), become mortal enemies because I think they are taking delight in my demise. Television commentators likewise. Remember how I described the whole of the MCG being against me? Having a good loud swear or breaking something precious are necessary to reach stage four: acceptance.

An odd one this because despite the unholy financial mess, a sense of calm will wash over. It is a relief of sorts that the battle with the bookmaker is finished. The fate is known. Besides, I will "never bet again … well, not at least for a couple of days" and "it could be worse, I could have terminal cancer". Gone are the evil thoughts of a couple of stages ago. A rueful chuckle may even pass the lips.

This lightening of the mood is essential for stage five. Recuperation. This may well be unique to yours truly. But after a particularly bad loss the pull to tell everyone and anyone all about it is huge. Walking away from a stadium I'll corner someone on the concourse, approach people in the queue at a hot dog stall, nudge someone in the ribs on the bus back to town or chase others down the road. "Come back! I want to tell you about how Andrew Symonds made me homeless!" Normally people will offer some sympathy. They will laugh about it. So will I. Then they'll ask why I did it. See stage one.

If I took my whole trip as a single wager, Melbourne was the stage when fear won out over expectation. Before I had arrived in Sydney, I was £1,002 short of my target, an insurmountable sum with confidence lower than Baz's chat-up technique and only a fifth Test, a casino and the pokies to do something about it. Certainly the casino option looked unattractive to say the least given it was responsible for the beginning of my implosion in Melbourne.

I discussed my options with Baz over his early morning cigarette and handful of health pills, helpfully pointing out the irony of his intake of lung-clogging smoke and all the vitamins of the alphabet. He was unequivocal that one should only bet on what one knows about.

"Think about it," he said, swallowing an earth-coloured tablet which looked like something which had dropped out of a large animal's backside. "You don't apply for a job that you don't know anything about so why would you gamble on something you know nothing about?"

I had caught Baz in his sensible work mode, the collar of his shirt preventing the blood from rushing to his head.

"I mean," he continued. "The people who bet on pokies are unfortunates – they've got addictive personalities. You shouldn't let a programme like the one the other night cloud your thinking."

"Yep, if it wasn't gambling it would be drugs or booze," I suggested.

"Right, I like a bet but I'm no addict."

"Me neither. A bet gives a nice feeling but it's no craving. I can't get addicted to something which is just 'nice'. It's like getting addicted to water skiing. Or sex."

"Man! Don't get me started," choked Baz, almost swallowing his fag. "Those sex addicts get on my tits. They're all celebrities. Just showing off, they are. We'd all be addicts if we could get laid as easily as them."

With that our high-brow discussion was over. Baz took a final drag from his cigarette and flicked it four storeys below on to the street. "Have a good day," he said.

I spent the next 30 minutes or so on the NSW government's advice site for problem gamblers. To read it was to be left in no doubt that the slot for your money on a pokie was a black hole. Quotes like "it does not make a difference whether you win by playing on certain days of the week or by pressing the buttons a certain way" gave an indication of the intelligence/desperation of the pokie player.

There was also the option of taking a tremendously amusing quiz to find out whether you had a problem. 'Congratulations! You've won a gambling addiction!'. The questions were all closed and were cannily phrased so it was virtually impossible to say 'no' to any of them. Questions two and five were particularly, like, 'duh!'

"Do you feel guilty about the way you gamble?" and "Do you find that when you stop gambling you've run out of money?" If you answer 'yes' to both of those, according to the site, gambling will be "causing real damage in your life" and you're an addict. You're not. You're a human being. Just the same as if there was a site set up to help, hmmm let's see, people addicted to food, posing "Are you often hungry when you haven't eaten for an hour or so?" or "sometimes, do you feel guilty about scoffing the last cookie in the jar?". I'd like to think the warning after questions such as these were tackled would read "You fat fuck! Stop eating before you collapse the world!"

Better questions to ask potential problem gamblers would be "do you steal from old grannies to pay for your addiction?" or "do you sell your personal possessions to pay for your addiction?" Actually, scrap that last one because that was exactly what I did in Melbourne.

The best part, however, was a gambling calculator which, by dint of an equation to make Pythagoras boss-eyed (asking for figures of how much you lost per gambling 'visit' and how much cash you withdrew to carry on), told you how much you would lose per year. I inputted my vital statistics from Melbourne and was told I would be down to the tune of 80 grand per annum.

Thanks for that.

After such a stark warning there was only one thing I could do. Go to the pub and bet. I took a stroll up Jones Bay Road, past the entrance to the Star City Casino, which with its black-window frontage looked like a giant mouth trying to suck me in, to the Point Bar. It was a liquor in the front, pokies in the back type of place, modelled on the sort of pubs back in the day when it was perfectly acceptable to go for a pint and a fight. The chairs were of the sort you would expect to see in a Western; strong enough to take the weight of a fair dinkum Aussie but flimsy enough to shatter on his head if he looked at your sheila the wrong way. The cricket was on one big screen, horseracing on the other, and there was a TAB betting facility in the corner. At the back, as I said, were the pokies. Ten altogether, flashing mischievously. If each of them took the average amount of cash per year for a Sydney pokie, the room would be worth $600,000. You would've thought they'd be able to afford better furniture

This is where the comeback would begin. Or so I hoped. I ordered myself an orange juice, sat in front of the television screen and took a deep breath as I prepared for the possibility of the emotional car crash that was stages one to five.

Bets 1 and 2

Back to basics. Remember Brisbane and all that stuff about how it was important to plan one's bets around the state of the ball? If it was new, expect wickets. If it was old expect runs. When Ian Bell and Kevin Pietersen were brought together with England two wickets down in the first innings of the match, it was about 20 overs old – the perfect time for batting to become easier. I bought the fall of the next England wicket at 98 for a couple of quid, which meant that so long as the two batsmen stayed at the crease and took England past that figure, I would win money. Anything below that and I would lose. If England lost their third wicket with the score on 110, I would win £24 (98-110 (=12) x2 =24) but if a wicket fell immediately (the score was 60) I would drop almost £100. I also backed Ian Bell to top score for £30. He often started like a Morris Minor in winter but once he got going he could chug along in the middle lane while all the flashier models spun off.

The spread bet was the sort of wager that could put you in a mental institution. With the target so far off, every ball was a panic attack. My heart would thump stronger and louder with every stride the bowler took towards the crease and when he released the ball, with my eye convinced it was zeroing in towards the batsman's stumps, I'm sure it would stop for a beat, catching up rapidly when it was all clear. Within ten minutes I thought the tension had caused me to go blind because my vision was blurred. Had I glaucoma? Was that even how you spelt it? I could barely see the screen. Deterioration rapid. Things…blurry… Panic over. A bit of the chocolate bar I had purchased had smudged on my spectacles.

The struggle between expectation and fear lasted for about an hour. Pietersen strolled down the wicket and biffed a ball for four to take England past the magical figure of 98. I had won out. It would now just be a question of how much I would win.

Going straight to the relief stage, I swaggered over to the bar to purchase a beer. My mood was enhanced when I watched a middle-aged Australian couple arguing about what horse they should back in race five at Moone Valley.

The woman was the sort you would take home to mother if you wanted to get hold of the inheritance early. She was wearing what could only be described as her grandfather's vest and had tattoos all up one arm. And she was adamant that a beast called Spunky Monkey was the one to back. Her man was having none of it.

"It's gotta be Radio City darl," he insisted.

"Na, na, na Clive, Spunky Monkey all the way. All the way," returned Miss Congeniality.

"Radio's got the form. Spunky Monkey's got zero," replied our

Clive, increasingly put out.

Unsurprisingly for a vest-wearing woman with a graffiti arm, she went nuts.

"I want Spunky Monkey Clive! Put the wad on Spunky now!" Clive, the bravest man on the planet, refused. Quietly and calmly he said: "It's Radio City. Look at the bloody form."

Clive may have been brave. But he was also stupid. Radio City came second. To Spunky Monkey.

The trauma which Clive was going through, and would continue to go through when his other half got him home, made my mind up that I should close my bet. Quit while you're ahead. At the tea break I was able to take a profit of £182.

I was back in the game in extraordinary fashion and strolled away from the Point Bar with the sun on my back and a cry of "It's Spunky Monkey!" ringing in my ears as Clive was set upon by his beau.

Bet 3

A former colleague of mine at *The Sportsman* kindly sorted me out with a ticket for day two at the Sydney Cricket Ground. He was in Sydney in his capacity as a business journalist for *The Daily Telegraph*. One of his contacts had a spare seat going. However, he warned me that I would be sitting next to an old English woman from the Home Counties who would not stop talking. He had complained that on day one she had been cooing over him because he was from Nottinghamshire and telling him anecdotes about Derek Randall, the former Notts batsman, which had no punchline whatsoever. "And I went to see him play and I was waving at him and crying out 'Derek! Derek!'" That was her best story.

When I arrived I made the situation clear. "Look love, no nattering. I've had a bloody big bet here and need to concentrate."

"Oooh, how interesting, tell me…"

"I'll stop you there. I need to win a lot of money, okay? You know how you get cold in the winter and moan to the council about your heating bill? Well, if I don't win here I won't be able to afford mine."

She didn't utter a word. Ian Bell failed to oblige but the heating bill looked like it would be paid thanks to a sell of England's runs at 370 for £3, netting a heart-warming £237.

Bet 4

I have no idea how Jesus Christ felt when he came back from the dead and all but I bet it was pretty close to the cockiness I felt before bet four. From just three wagers I had smashed back into contention with a profit of £389. No wonder JC had the muscle to move that ruddy great boulder blocking his resting place. I could have pushed over, er, a mountain or something when a sell of England second-innings runs collected a further £215. Alas my king-like status did not last long. I had failed to take into account the outstanding bets struck when optimism was ripe in the Brisbane air so many weeks ago. Those winnings were immediately wiped out when the £125 I had spent on England winning a Test and the £70 on Shane Warne being top Australia wicket-taker were accounted for. When someone asks me when I am an old man, "Did you see the greatest spinner of all time play? What was he like?" I will reply: "He was average. Overrated. Cost me money in 2007."

I had failed. Not by a measly few quid. But by almost half. A slim £707 was all I had to show after two months of almost non-stop gambling. That would cover the mortgage for about a month and 20 minutes. Okay, I was in profit but a target was a target and I had come up short. My quest was over. So were the Ashes. I was mightily relieved about both. Watching the majority of each Test had been like visiting five different cinemas, each miles from each other, to watch the same movie. You knew how it started, you knew exactly how it was going to end.

Over a cold beer on Baz's balcony, we dissected a 5-0 series whitewash for England and my immediate concerns about how I was going to prevent the repossession of my home on the return home. Baz, with his collar loosened, had little sympathy.

"The problem with your cricketers and your gambling is that you haven't been aggressive enough. You've got to sledge, get in people's faces." His point over my gambling was a metaphorical one (questioning the parentage of a casino croupier would not have done my cause any good) and valid. But he was way wide of the mark when it came to the cricket.

"Are you seriously suggesting England have lost 5-0 because they didn't do enough swearing?"

"Absolutely," said Baz.

"You're mad. They lost 5-0 because Australia had two of the best bowlers [Warne and Glenn McGrath] of all time in their side at the same time."

"No mate," he continued. "It's all about attitude. You gotta give 'em the stare, throw 'em a few insults, call their wife a slag."
I couldn't believe what I was hearing. That shirt collar must have been really tight.

"You're talking rubbish," I told him.

"I'm not. I'm playing cricket in a couple of days and I'm gonna be one mean sonofabitch. Just like the other 21 players. You English are soft."

A day later, Baz and I strolled down to a patch of grass by Darling Harbour with a bat and ball for what I thought would be a casual knock around. He had insisted I help him prepare for his match. The setting was idyllic. The sun was out and it seemed a perfect way for me to bring my journey to an end. Baz wanted to bat first.

"I'll start off with some gentle leg spinners," I told him as I ambled back to the stumps (my jumper).

Baz's eyes lit up at my first delivery. He swung brutishly to leg, sending the cricket ball (that's right, genuine hard ball) through the Sydney air like an Exocet missile. It narrowly missed a woman with a pushchair, which I presumed had a baby in (I couldn't see, it was that far away) and into two lanes of traffic.

Baz strutted down the wicket, not even looking at the 'pitch' as he jabbed it with his bat in the style of the professionals until he was about two inches away from my face. "Soft," he whispered.

"Maybe," I replied. "But you have just lost the ball."

Baz could have done with the practice. As I waited at the airport to catch my flight home, he called me to tell me how he got on in the game he played in.

"Out for a duck," he said. "Wasn't aggressive enough."

Distance travelled: 24,150km
Won: £1,825
Lost: £1,118
Profit/loss: +£707
Target: £1,300

Chapter 9
Pakistan

One of the great advantages of being a gambler is knowing about odds, which is why if you ever catch me buying a ticket for the national lottery, with the chances of winning the jackpot a measly one in 14 million, feel free to put my balls in a bingo machine. It allows me to be smug, you see. For example while most airline passengers will work themselves into a frenzy about the plane going into the ground like a dart, gripping their armrest as if it's a winning ticket and their faces going white like they've just seen the dog chew up the life-changing voucher, I can sit quite content knowing there are far more dangerous activities. And mock them for it. It was the only reason to make me smile at the prospect of a 24-hour flight back from Sydney to London and a well-earned betting break.

At that point I had placed my life in the hands of six different airline captains. During those journeys I developed a solid ruse to increase the tension of my fellow passengers. Feigning nervousness to my neighbour on take-off, I would stare at them with a wide-eyed look on my face and when they returned the favour, thumb towards the window, and mouth, "Does that look right to you?" Generally the odds are pretty short that they will go nuts.

Having said that, a friend of mine, who also happens to have one of the most highly-regarded of betting brains, gets in a terrible state about the whole business of flying. He only has himself to blame. He will watch Air Crash Investigation on television back-to-back for hours on one of those cable channels which has nothing else to show, phone me up and say "Did you know a plane over South America a few years back just dropped out of the bloody sky because some lazy groundstaff bloke forgot to put a piece of masking tape on the fuselage? That's it, I'm never getting on one of those things again."

"But why?" I will reply. "The odds of your plane crashing are millions to one."

"Yeah, but what are the chances of the bloody masking tape getting blown off?"

According to the National Safety Council in America the actual odds of your plane falling out of the sky on a single trip are one in 52.6 million. So you could say they are in your favour. You are more likely to die in a car accident, with odds of one in 7.6 million. In fact, and this really will stop you worrying, there is more of a likelihood of being killed after being bitten or struck by a dog, (yes, actually hit, presumably by a Boxer) than dying in a plane crash. Those odds stand at one in 120,000. Again our boffin buddies from across the pond have provided this information and given the average American is, of course, a bit of a ninny take it with a pinch of salt. Grab the whole cellar when you consider that there is a one in 1.5 million chance of dying by ignition or melting of nightwear. Setting your pyjamas on fire, basically. Clearly some American husband and wife combinations have taken the advice of the marriage counsellor to "put the spark back in the bedroom" literally.

"Oh my God honey! You're so hot!"

"Thanks cup cake, I try my best."

"You're on fire!"

"I aim to please."

"No, you are *actually* on fire!"

So next time you get on a plane do so with confidence. Unless that is, of course, two of your fellow passengers are a married American couple who are arguing a lot, wearing pyjamas and have a Boxer dog with them.

What should be feared is boredom. And I was terrified of the thought of a whole day in the air, easily the longest journey of my adventure, with only a short stopover at Singapore. A mind-numbing is far more disconcerting than an arse-numbing brought on by sitting with shoulders hunched forward, head bowed as if impersonating a squirrel, pinching the free nuts into your mouth which are only an 'appetiser' for the 'meal' which you will eat from the head of the sweaty bloke in front while wondering "mmm, perhaps this is what cancer tastes like" and breathing in 500 fellow travellers' recycled flatulence.

Then I saw the stewardess and was quite happy to stay cooped up forever in a flying fart box. I had been told that the female 'flight attendants', to give them their correct title, on Singapore Airlines were beautiful. So beautiful that you would give your right arm to take one out on a date and yet when she saw you were minus one limb and told you 'she wasn't in to that sort of thing' you wouldn't mind in the least, reckoning a lifetime of disability was a worthy sacrifice. This woman's hip bones kinked with such definition when she walked that she could have knocked off the tops of beer bottles with each glorious step. Left stride, ping! Right stride, ping! Beer everywhere.

There and then I declared to give up gambling for her. After all, she was from Singapore and was probably against it. I would recount the story in my speech at our wedding about how we met, how she changed my mad monetary ways ending with a joke of which the punchline would be "…and then she asked to see my landing gear. Arf!" and everyone would fall about laughing.

Despite being aware that my chances with this picture of loveliness were somewhere between being struck to death by an argumentative dog who blamed himself for his owner's divorce and igniting like a chip pan in a pyromaniac's kitchen the next time I dressed for bed, I thought I was on to a winner.

This was only fuelled when she kept bringing me stuff, a sure way of stealing my heart. Whenever a woman provides me with something, I fancy them. It must be a maternal thing. Food, drink – which put waitresses and bar girls in particular danger – dead pigeon. I'll take it and try to get their number. Within 15 minutes the sumptuous stewardess had brought me a blanket, a cushion, socks, a toothbrush, headphones, pipe and slippers. Okay, I made the last two up but it was like Christmas. 'God, I'm in! This is so easy it's not even fair'. Then I noticed she was handing the same gifts out to everyone.

Unperturbed, I decided to press on. It would occupy the mind. When she brought me my seafood with pasta and vegetable salad followed by stir-fried pork with spring onions and seasonal vegetables, I would look at her name tag. Get the name. Always a prerequisite. Could I get away with smelling her, too? Or was that too risky? One step at a time, my boy. Name first, sniff later. Always a prerequisite.

While straining my eyes to clock her name tag she mistakenly thought I was staring at her breasts and fixed me with a look as if I had just asked if I could score smack off her little sister. The wedding of the year looked almost certainly a non-starter when I had to wait longer for my main course than everyone else and I was mysteriously the only person not to be given an ice-cream. Given that incident, I am perhaps not the best to give advice on courting. But this is an area where knowledge of betting and odds can be very useful. Now is an opportune time to explain why finding a winning horse is a lot like winning a woman. For a start, and if you will forgive me for being a little direct, what we are all really looking for is a good ride. So off we go down to the paddock to look at what is on offer. Ideally, we don't want to go after the favourite because that will be the first choice of everyone. Gait and muscle tone are important as is spotting something only a few others may go for, but not one which is so awful looking that people will not think you are a bit of a shrewdie when you make your selection. Then decide how much you want to invest and prepare to spend the rest of your time muttering "stupid mare".

If you have found yourself a winning woman, you could do worse than take her on a long-haul flight for a first date because such a trip is like two or three dates rolled into one. Or in extreme cases, a whole relationship because by the time you have got off and had the obligatory row at the luggage carousel, you never want to see each other again. But when you are actually on the plane, you can watch a film with your squeeze, enjoy a three-course meal and then you get to sleep with them afterwards, although not in a biblical sense. Also, there is absolutely no chance of her storming out.

By the time I had worked out this dating option, and risked being slapped with a restraining order from an offended stewardess, it was time to get off at Singapore.

Back on board even the choice of 80 films, innumerable rubbish comedy shows, computer games, the flight tracker system which told me exactly where the plane was and its route, and the option of learning a new language – there were 21 with Tamil the most exotic – my brain started to hurt with boredom. Briefly I amused myself by using the linguistic learning option to work out what "I did my bollocks in Melbourne" translated into but I could only manage French and German. Still it didn't stop me declaring in that loud voice which people use only when they are wearing headphones "j'ai fait mes testicules à Melbourne!" and "ich tat meine hoden in Melbourne!" several times before I was told by the object of my unrequited love that other passengers were trying to sleep. She definitely didn't fancy me.

So I left the slumber zone and headed to the back of the plane where the old age pensioners spend virtually the whole journey stretching their limbs to prevent deep vein thrombosis. There was only one in position, however, raising his arm and leg as if attempting a Nazi salute and goose step at the same time. He looked ridiculous, particularly because even in the gloom of the cabin lights I could see he had on the top of his head, possibly the most obvious wig ever. Clearly this was someone I had to talk to.

"Boring isn't it, this travel lark?" I offered.

"What did you soi there?" he shouted back in an unmistakable Birmingham accent, which seemed odd because his ears were not covered by any headphones. "I'm sorroi to shout! But I'm a bit dif!"

Turning up the volume myself, I replied: "These long-haul plane journeys, boring aren't they?"

He gave me a look as if he had found his soulmate, rolled his eyes and in a now-familiar bellow replied: "Ow yes. I've done a lot of travelling and I joost hate the flying. This is the last one for moi. Never again."

Before I was able to ask him about the sights he had seen in his globetrotting days, Miss Hip Bones, with one kink narrowly missing a small child which connection would have resulted in the little one going into orbit, strutted down the aisle, and told us to stop shouting. I really was going to have to make a remarkable recovery to score from here.

"Sorry, he's a bit deaf," I explained.

"Sorrroi, I'm a bit dif!" hollered my new pal. "I can't hear above the noise of the en-gins!"

Miss Hips allowed herself a laconic puff of her perfect cheeks (the ones on her face), uninterested in getting involved in a row with a man who only a few hours before had almost suffered cataract damage ogling her chest and another who wouldn't even be able to hear her point of view. So we were left to shout at each other quite happily for an hour or so, during which time I discovered Keith was from Solihull, was 68 years old, had a wife called Mary or "Mare-roi" as he called her, was a miserable so and so and had done an awful lot of travelling, that is when he could remember where he had gone. I thought he was great. Much of our conversation time was spent on me offering place names in response to his rhetorical question "now, where was it we went that year?" or just looking like a spare part when he thought long and hard about this particular poser: "Was it foive holidays a year for the last six years or six holidays a year for the last foive?"

Once we discovered where and when he had gone, he was terrific.

"Ow! Don't go to Borneo. Twenty-eight hours to git there and it was bloody roobish. Not worth it. Went for the bloody woildlife but all I saw were four oranga-tans and they were in a zoo. One was called George ... Kenya, saw all the woildlife. Too much if you ask me. Not a safe place. They think you're filthy rich yow see... Mauritius. Oh! Don't get me started. Too many su-ga canes!"

After a brief period trying to discover whether Mare-roi and he had been on a cruise to Norway ("they all had blond hair") or the Caribbean ("actually it was too hot for Norway") or Panama ("there was a big canal") we got on to the subject of my gambling gambol.

"I've been ploying Super Mario Broothers to beat the boredom and got quite good. A foiver to the bloke who can get furthest on the first level," he offered.

I didn't know what was more astonishing; being offered a wager several thousand feet in the air by a geriatric or the fact that this man knew who Super Mario was. Keith, truly, was a find. It is not often I would be 50-50 to beat a 68-year-old, who doesn't know where he has been or is going, at a computer game which was invented for my generation, so I accepted. And before you start having qualms about taking money off the old and having visions about Keith and Mare-roi freezing to death after being unable to pay the central heating bill, remember the pair have been able to afford five holidays in the past six years. Or six in the past five.

Keith's memory loss not only extended to the countries he had visited. It also included his ability at Super Mario Brothers. He was no good. He lasted just five seconds on the easiest level first time so I felt sorry for him and let him have another go. He managed to keep going for 12 seconds. "Okay, Keith. Pay up. We'll have a rematch before we land," I said as he handed me the cash and headed back to my seat, feeling pleased that I had not even managed to get through a long-haul flight without having a bet.

Contentment only increased when discovering on the flight tracker that Keith and I had actually placed our bet when we were flying over Pakistan. Now I know betting is illegal there so on that basis I was pretty sure that the ban extended to their airspace, too.

Pakistan would have been an interesting place to visit for the purpose of this book because, despite gambling being outlawed, it was rife. However, I didn't fancy it; firstly because with my boyish good looks and blond locks, I was convinced that I would be kidnapped, made to wear an orange jump suit and paraded on the internet in grainy images quicker than you could say "Al-Qaeda" and secondly I had done a bit of research into the Islamic state and was not particularly attracted by the mass of contradictions. For a country who the majority believe women are sacred it is a trifle more than double standards to have upheld laws which demand that any woman who claims she has been raped, must produce four witnesses to the crime. Otherwise it is adultery, which is a big no-no in Islam. And the punishment? Stoning.

Unsurprisingly rape is increasingly taking on hobby status for Pakistani men. You may find this gripe a bit rich coming from a chap who has just compared women to horses and suggest that in no way am I qualified to start degrading the Muslim faith, something which is increasingly taking on hobby status for Westerners. You are probably right but even using gambling as a search tool there are incidents uncovered which will ensure that efforts to promote tourism – Visit Pakistan 2007 had just been launched by the prime minister – and to stop people like me looking at the country through a blindfold are likely to flounder. In November 2005 in a town in Punjab a gambling dispute got so out of control that three churches, two houses of priests, one convent, one high school and the houses of three Christian families were set alight by a 2,500-strong Muslim mob. The reason for the rampage occurred the day before. A Christian cattle trader was playing cards with a Muslim when an argument erupted – nothing particularly unusual about that. However, the

Christian, according to Muslims, was unable to control his anger and set fire to copies of the Qur'an. In Islam this is considered blasphemy, probably the biggest no-no going. Christians said the Muslim invented the whole story to distract attention from his whopping gambling debts. The result was Muslims working themselves into a frenzy, going on a vandalism rampage because of the sacrilege and conveniently forgetting that had one of their kin been applying the letter of the law of the land in the first place, there would have been no need to start setting fire to stuff. See what I mean about contradiction? The inconsistencies continue. Virtually at the same time as we were flying over Pakistan a mother – remember how precious women are in Islam – was appealing for help from authorities because her daughter was being claimed by a man as payment of a 16-year-old gambling debt. Nooran Bibi said her late husband had promised her daughter, Rasheeda, to one Lal Haider in lieu of poker liabilities amounting to 10,000 rupees, about £80. Roughly the equivalent of three nights' stay in Pooraka's Pavlos Motel.

And in the wake of the death of Pakistan cricket coach Bob Woolmer in March 2007, which had been linked to a match-fixing mafia, Imran Khan*, the former Test captain, said the country had descended into such a state of lawlessness that attempts to quash corruption in the game and close down illegal gambling houses were like "treating cancer with Dispirin". He went on to explain how efforts to shut 53 gambling schools and brothels in Lahore faltered when the addresses given to police were traced back to members of the ruling party.

My favourite incongruity involves good old Imran himself, who after throwing away his whites became a politician in Pakistan and in 2006 had a not-particularly-well-read column in a gambling newspaper in England, which had the tagline "the racing and sports betting daily". I know that because I was his ghost writer.

The problem may be that the Qur'an, the central religious text of Islam and life guide if you will, is somewhat of a contradiction itself because your religious extremists (those with long beards) will interpret chunks of it to support their argument while the moderates (those with slightly shorter ones) will read the same parts and do likewise. Take this small piece of advice from the Prophet Muhammad as a case in point:

> *They ask you [Prophet] about intoxicants and gambling: say, "There is great sin in both, and some benefit for people: the sin is greater than the benefit." They ask you what they should give: say, "Give what you can spare."*

Even devout Muslims admit they are unsure whether Muhammad has partly permitted drinking and gambling or condemned it. Personally, I reckon he is giving some of the soundest betting advice ever uttered; if you are a winning punter, carry on. If not, best give it up, pal. Later on in the sacred book, a tougher line is taken:

> *With intoxicants and gambling, Satan seeks only to incite enmity and hatred among you, and to stop you remembering God and prayer. Will you not give them up?*

Notice this time that believers are only being asked to give up gambling. There is no suggestion that you burn for all eternity if you fancy trap three in the 2.30pm at Monmore. Admittedly there may be a verse here or chapter there tucked away which specifically precludes having a wager, but, to be frank, it is a bit of an arduous read and given that cleverer brows than mine have furrowed at its content, that will do for me. Certainly from those two examples it seems something of a leap of faith to not only ban it completely but to mete out a damn good flogging to anyone caught doing it.

In short then, I was glad we were making haste above Pakistan and heading home to London. I wondered if Keith would be interested in discussing the labyrinthine world of Pakistani politics.

"You do know we had our bet over Pakistan, don't you, which is, if we're going to be real sticklers, probably illegal," I told him.

"Ow!" he exclaimed. "Don't get me started! Pakistan, bloody roobish. Me and Mare-roi… oh hang on, was it Rajasthan?"

*A major high-street bookmaker is keeping a nervous eye on Imran's political career. They laid a 16-1 bet to members of the Goldsmith family that at some time in his life, Imran becomes prime minister of Pakistan. The bookmaker in question is extremely worried for two reasons; one, the PM role is so easy to get they may as well give it away if you collect the right number of tokens from a cereal box, and two, it will cost them a six-figure sum.

Distance travelled: 41,315km
Won: £1,830
Lost: £1,118
Profit/loss: +£712
Target: £1,300

Chapter 10
Home

They say that the definition of anti-climax is to reckon you are the world's greatest lover only to discover your wife suffers from asthma. It's not true. It is to return to England following a failed global gambling adventure, the once golden leaves under foot now nothing more than grey skeletons, and to open the door of your homestead to find your flatmate showering fully clothed in a linen suit.

"What on earth are you doing?"

"New money saving plan," said Flatmate. "Boiler's broken you see, saves on dry cleaning."

"I see," I mused. "Is that why it's so cold in here?"

"Ya! Pretty cold in here too."

Once Flatmate had hung up his soaking suit, dried off, telephoned his mobile phone company because someone was sending him websites with "pictures of women in the state of undress", put the kettle on, and moaned I had not brought any biscuits back, he remembered.

"Did you reach the target?"

"No, short by almost half."

"Cripes! Boilers aren't cheap you know."

It was all rather depressing. I should have been welcomed like some returning hero. Where was the red carpet? The dancing girls? Or just the girls? Instead I got a posh, drowned prat nervously telling someone in a mobile phone call centre: "Look,

I, er, don't know, ah, how to put this but, the, er, images, shall we say, are unclean."

It was hard to adjust. Harder still to work out how, without a full-time job, I would be able to keep the repo men from knocking on my door. Once jet lag had passed, I set about sending off CVs and cover letters to find work, phoning old friends for favours, even considering working in a bar because I had some misguided romantic image of me throwing cocktail shakers around the place in front of adoring blondes.

I went to the job centre, too; a trip which proved to be the most singularly depressing and frustrating experience of my life. I filled out, ooh I don't know, about 20 forms and then waited for two hours to see a woman intent on taking out the fact that she was going through the menopause on her computer keyboard. She torpedoed her fingers into the keys, refusing to look at me as she inputted my data.

"Have you ever received compensation for an injury sustained during World War Two?" she asked.

"Yes," I said.

She glared at me.

"Sorry my mistake," I countered. "I thought you said World War One."

When it came to searching for work similar to my previous position, she insisted on looking on her database for 'cricket tipster'. I tried to reason with her that this was a waste of time because the employment opportunities for such a role were limited to say the least.

"But you don't know," she bristled. "You don't know what I've got on my computer."

"Look," I said. "I'm pretty sure there won't be a job for a cricket tipster. There were only two of those jobs in the world four months ago and there is only one now."

"I'm searching for cricket tipster jobs, sir."

Long pause.

"There aren't any. Listen, our first role here is to see if we can find you work in the sector or field that you previously worked in. For your next consultancy we'll look at other options. Come back next week."

I didn't bother to go back next week. Instead I got a gig writing travel guides to German cities for an in-flight magazine having travelled across the country extensively in 2005, the highlight of which was being invited to a house party in Cologne thrown by the chap who played David Brent in the German version of *The Office*. No, he didn't do the dance.

This allowed me to work from home, a new and strange experience. On the one hand it was good because I had the time to do all the little chores I'd been putting off for ages: fix that squeaky floorboard, paint my bedroom, clean out the fridge. On the other it was bad because doing all the little chores prevented me from doing any work.

Plus, there was the cabin fever. The average male speaks 7,000 words a day. I was managing about 70. Cooped up with only four walls to stare at, reality becomes a mirage, social skills disappear quicker than snot down the plughole. When I did meet an 'outsider', for weeks I thought it was immensely amusing, and acceptable, to reply when asked 'what do you do?' with: "Sit at home, drink tea, eat cake, watch porn."

The few occasions I did go out into the big wide world was to join the ranks of the casual newspaper sub-editors working for national publications. Aside from the money being pretty darn good, it was disheartening.

'Surely not, you say. Journalists? Together? Shining the blade of truth to cut deeper? What laughs, what japes, what bonhomie! What bollocks. The casual sub-editor is the lowest of the low in newspaper circles. Full-time staff members, wary that you would probably kill them to take their job, would not use you to scrape dog poo off their shoe. And God forbid if you ever made the mistake of offering one of them a cheery 'good afternoon' at the start of a shift.

At one newspaper I worked for, about 12 sub-editors, half

staff and half casual, would sit in silence for nine hours, each side warily eyeing the other. On the one occasion that a staff member did speak to me, I thought I had broken through. Could it be that I would be allowed into the 'circle of trust'?

"Could I borrow a pound for a cup of tea, please, there's a good chap?" asked one of the two staffers that I was sharing a desk. I couldn't get the money out quick enough. He returned with two cups of tea. One for himself and one for the other staffer sat opposite. I didn't even get my change.

I am not ashamed to say that in the days and weeks after my return from my travels, I went slightly doolally, thanks to the experiences like the one I have just described when I did leave the flat. When the in-flight magazine was not pressing me for the price of a herrengedeck in the HappyHappyDingDong bar in Dortmund, I could be found at the dining room table with a slightly deranged look in my eye, while I leafed through the job pages to send off spoof applications for positions I was wholly unqualified for. It killed the time.

Dear Sir/Madam,

Apologies for my tardy application for Bathroom Designer at Ripples (Guardian 5/02/07) but I have been working myself into a lather rather.

It is, you see, my dream job. Bathrooms, and all what goes on in them, are my passion.

Indeed they have been ever since I was a teenager and my parents invited a B&Q saleswoman to our home to design us a sparkling new ablution adventure park.

It is with great excitement that I recall spending hours in there, working myself into a frenzy at the B&Q woman's mouldings and accessories.

Ever since I have been obsessed with bathrooms, lavatories, powder rooms, restrooms, saunas, shower rooms, steam rooms… well, you get the picture, although please note that I have not mentioned wet rooms, which I feel are a curse on bathroom culture and are just another example of society going down the pan by 'dumbing down'.

My desire for all things salle de bains, as the French call them, has helped me gain the qualifications you require.

My communication and sales skills were honed working in the B&Q (yes, I owe them a lot) bathroom section in Reading. I have an example of my gift of the gab, if you will. Keith, a rather simpleton colleague of mine at B&Q, was not such a good talker and often repeated the mistake of answering "of course I bloody do, it's January 17" when asked by a customer "do you have a bidet?"

I was able to help Keith and B&Q by informing the manager of his inexperience and he was removed from his position, thus helping Keith find his real calling in life.

As for me I have progressed to designing my own bathrooms. I have been busy working on my 'showroom', which is my own bathroom.

I passionately believe that fine bathrooms should be available to all so I have structured my design technique around affordable accessories, or to put it another way, ones you can make yourself. For example I have borrowed my sister's baby pram to make a replica of the Argento vanity unit by Bianchini & Capponi. As you know this retails at nearly £6,000 but mine has cost pence thanks to the wonder of tinfoil. Unfortunately my sister needs the pram back next week.

Other ingenious money-saving design techniques include using an every-day kitchen colander to replicate the Hansgrohe Raindance Rainmaker, which is the largest shower head in the world.

Hopefully my specialty once you offer me the job would be to show customers how to save thousands of pounds by making beautiful bathrooms from what they find lying around in boxes in the garage.

Together we could make waves, not just Ripples (!!!!!)

Best washes (another pun)

Signed

PS: I failed to mention my drawing skills, which are first class. I have a GCSE 'C' grade in Art.

You feel for me I'm sure. I recovered my faculties about a week later when Ripples got in contact to ask whether I fancied coming in for an interview. Yes, honestly. However, when I replied with the letter below, strangely I didn't hear from them again…

Dear Madam,

Well, you could have knocked me down with a plunger.
I'd be delighted to meet you – we could chuck some ideas into the hot tub, press the 'Go' button and see what rises to the surface.
I would also like to show you plans for the homemade Jacuzzi, which puts to good use an unloved Electrolux hoover (Genius, I know. I surprise myself some times!). Perhaps Ripples could produce them and sell in store?
There have been teething problems I admit. Installation did not go too well yesterday and I flooded the downstairs flat. They were furious. I offered to build one for them as compensation but they were just not having it.
Therefore I've been unable to bathe or shower since. So when I come to see you I'll need to use the facilities in your showroom. I'll bring soap but all my towels have been used to mop up. Can you provide?

Yours sink-cerely (pun)

signed

PS: Do you want me to bring my Bianchini & Capponi basin/ pram? It's still got its wheels!

My trip back into the land of the lucid began with a most unexpected call from an extremely polite and charming chap called David Edwards. He was the sports editor of *The London Paper*, a free sheet handed out to help pass the time on the Underground, and he wanted little old me to write a regular column where I would go to train with sporting superstars and make a fool of myself.

"Can you do that?" he asked.

"You bet."

Not only did this job get me out of the flat, it got me talking to people again and I was getting paid into the bargain. I was the living embodiment of the phrase 'throw like a girl' with the London United basketball team, came 75th in the World Crazy Golf Championships, and in a tennis knock-up with infamous hothead John McEnroe, I told him "I'm going to call your shots out all the time, just to see if I can get up your nose." Superbrat ignored me, disgusted at the suggestion of his shots going anywhere near the white line or me even returning the ball. He was right. McEnroe was statuesque in the centre of the court, pinging the ball left and right with that familiar shot-making artistry and deft volleys to have me running from one side to the other like a cowed messenger scurrying nervously from the wrath of his king. He was good. But we knew that. What was impressive about the guy was his aura. It literally hummed in the air. It needed its own space in the car park. And its own hotel room.

Expletive-leaden incredulity was the response I got from a tennis nut pal when I told him I was having a knock-up with McEnroe. You lucky so-and-so was the printable version. But the seven-time grand slam winner did not just cause awe-spluttering wonderment in the average Joe.

Rugby's Jonny Wilkinson, hardly an underachiever, shared a stage with McEnroe at this press junket and was reduced to a gibbering wreck: "You can be in a room full of people and McEnroe walks in and everyone goes 'oh my God'." Wilkinson was right. By the way Australian cricketers Brett Lee and Adam Gilchrist were also present, but no-one really noticed them, tucked away somewhere in the shadows created by that McEnroe ego.

"He can affect people's lives without opening his mouth." Wilkinson again. Not quite, Jonny, one thought, although McEnroe's magic was working fine when just a few hours after he said that Andy Murray couldn't win Wimbledon this year, the Scot pulled out.

I also played darts against a living legend.

Most blokes would give their right arm to challenge multiple world champion Phil 'The Power' Taylor. How they would expect to throw the arrers is anyone's guess but then Taylor, arguably Britain's greatest sportsman, had that effect on people; opponents are often starstruck to the extent that their limbs do odd things.

Not me, though. My fascination was the contradiction of these terrifically fat chaps being so highly skilled. And how when one of them tried to lose weight – Taylor had been on a diet – he loses form. When I met him at the Princess Alice pub in Aldgate, I was keen for him to explain. Unfortunately I could not get a word in. Taylor talked about anything but darts. The number of houses he had bought for his family, his sports trophies and memorabilia shop in Stoke, why he imported polo shirts from China, embroidery and how camera equipment is cheaper in Holland.

"Let's play darts!" I boomed. It was all I could do to stop myself prodding him with one of his tungsten tools.

"Sure," he smiled before explaining how he uses his right shoulder as his guide and the importance of transferring weight to the front foot. Then with that familiar wide-eyed look and his lips puckered as if about to sip a drink, he went quiet. And fired three arrers into the board for a 180.

Then he was off again. "It's like a golf swing, you've got to follow through… you're an army sniper firing a gun. Peow! Peow! … you're a boxer, look at me, and you're only throwing half a jab. You'll get knocked out, Eddie."

Unsure whether to swing, shoot or punch I still managed to land three darts near the treble 20. "Yeah, baby. You're a boxer," Taylor said as he approached and mock body-punched me three or four times in the ribs. "In the world championships I keep hitting 'em, never let up, batter 'em."

"Phil," I asked. "Do you talk this much when you are on the oche?"

"Nope," he replied. "I stay silent. Let the pressure get to them."

"Probably for the best," I said.

Taylor did speak some sense during our meeting. He spoke of the need to practise, practise. And then practise some more. It struck a chord.

Taylor wanted to be the best he could possibly be at darts. So he worked hard. I wanted to be the best sporting chancer I could possibly be. So I went off on a jolly to Australia and then moaned that I had underperformed. My gambling skills had to be honed further if I was to make a good living. I needed to practise, practise. And then practise some more. Taylor had again ignited the fire in my belly after it had been doused by a dose of the grumps and feeling sorry for myself.

I had the urge to challenge myself once more and set about canvassing the opinions of the great and the good of the gambling world. 'What were the three qualities a gambler could not do without?' Most of them said 'lots of money' but let's ignore that. The three which kept cropping up were: Discipline. Emotional detachment. Luck. I got the atlas out again, the travel books and the world map of terror. I needed to find three places where the above precious commodities could be tested.

Chapter 11
Discipline – Las Vegas

It takes nine-and-a-half hours to fly to Las Vegas from London, giving you plenty of time to come to terms with the fact that when you arrive, you will succumb to either the betting, the booze or the birds. But more likely all three.

Las Vegas gets you in the end. It is a city built on sin, capable of eroding the morals of a saint, literally: the first settlers on this patch of Nevada desert in 1855 were the Mormons who, as self-proclaimed Latter Day Saints, were not keen on the betting, the booze or the birds.

If more than 150 years later the descendants of those Mormons could not keep their discipline and oppose laws to legalise gambling, 24-hour drinking and prostitution, what chance does the average Joe Schmoe have? None. Although plenty step off the plane reckoning they can look temptation in the eye and not blink first. The percentage of visitors who say they are not coming to gamble is 95 per cent. The percentage of visitors who end up gambling is 87 per cent. And we're not talking about just a couple of dollars in a slot machine here and a few dollars on roulette there. Las Vegas wears the non-believers down to an average time at the tables of a whopping four hours a day.

All this perhaps should be taken lightly. After all, these are Americans we are talking about. A fifth of them can't even locate their own country on a map so there is a strong chance a fair chunk of Yanks stepping off a jet in Vegas merely popped out to buy a loaf of bread, took a wrong turn and ended up in the gambling capital of the globe. Still, once in Vegas, albeit by accident, they love it. And why wouldn't they? An American friend once boasted to me that "in a country where everything is bigger, brasher and better, Vegas is where Americans go to be impressed". That does not mean the rest of us have to be. Just like a magpie's eye is taken by something gold or shiny-looking, I had visions of Americans in Vegas standing transfixed, open-mouthed with drool escaping down one side like that leaking tap in the bathroom you've been meaning to get fixed for ages. The toytown, fantasy feel of a city with a Statue of Liberty, mini Eiffel Tower, Sphinx, rare white Bengal tigers prowling a few feet away from the tables and topless showgirls re-enacting the sinking of the Titanic ('Quick! Grab on to these, there are no life jackets left!') was designed for the cerebrally challenged.

That much is clear from the view of the monopoly-board layout of the Strip from the plane window on approach to McCarran airport. The Circus Circus casino with its giveaway big-top landmark at one end and Excalibur, a medieval themed one at the other, perfectly summed up the jollification and largesse of the playground below. It is about this time one should remember the advertising slogan for the city, which is 'what happens in Vegas, stays in Vegas'. Or in other words 'what money you happen to take to Vegas, stays in Vegas'. The jingle is a work of smarts for the way it entices all manner of industries to hold their trade fairs and conferences with the faux promise of immunity for their attendees from any high jinks, conveniently glossing over the racing certainty that very, very little work will get done.

That spanner you've been waiting for yonks to arrive in the post to fix the faulty tap discussed earlier? Blame the Speciality Tools and Fasteners Distribution Association who hold their annual conference there. Peeved with the shoddy work done on your new driveway? The World of Concrete Expo took place in January. Fed up with pigeons pooing on your head and getting splinters in your backside from that dodgy rocking chair while trying to watch an episode of *Countdown*? The International Roofing Expo was in town followed by the Woodworking and Furniture Suppliers Fair. Distraught at how the floral tribute for the cremation of uncle Fred was misspelt with an extra vowel in the worst possible place? Before the year would be out the National Funerals Directors' Association were due to let their hair down.

I was to visit during one of the more hedonistic periods in the Vegas calendar for the World Series of Poker. Not that I was complaining. By a matter of days I missed the World Shoe Association's annual conference (would the home of the shoe, Northampton, not have been a better choice?), which was attended by people standing around talking cobblers, who are most certainly not the life and sole of the party and, wait for it, deserve a good kicking.

My experience of poker is similar to that of world shoe conferences: limited. I took part in a media event before the 2005 Ashes series, but really I was way out of my depth. I had a brief study up of how the game worked but by the time I took my seat at a table I had forgotten everything. Thinking 'sod it, I'll just happily chat away to the chap on my left instead of attempting to fathom what was happening', I found myself doing rather well. Every time it was my turn to call, raise or check, I had to stop nattering, look at my cards and make my decision. Invariably I raised a shrug of the shoulders and an indifferent toss of the chips. My fellow players took this casual demeanour as a sign of a crack player. All I had to do was grab a handful and people would fold.

Chap to my left was mightily impressed. His name was Colin 'Funky' Miller, a former Australia Test cricketer who was more famous for dyeing his hair all the colours of the carnival rather than being any good. His chum to his left was even more impressed. "Jeez mate, you're a good player," said Merv Hughes, a terrifying Aussie quick bowler who had also conducted his own interesting hair experiment (he had a huge walrus-style moustache).

Miller soon fell for the ruse and Hughes, who was trying to put me off by telling jokes involving two blokes in a sauna, one with a hare lip and the other with water on the brain, was my next victim. Soon a crowd had gathered to watch this ice-cool player who had accounted for two infamous and uncompromising antipodeans without, apparently, even concentrating. Eventually me and a guy, who was obviously taking it seriously because he wore a shirt with a logo of aces and was wearing sunglasses (he could have been blind but I thought it unlikely), were the only two left. I went through the same routine but old blindy wouldn't budge. It came to the point where we both had to turn our cards over. At which point the crowd gasped. So did blindy. So I did likewise. He shook his head. Likewise. And then he extended his hand and said "well played. Nice suit." I wasn't even wearing one. Without at any stage knowing the meaning of the cards in my hand or those on the table, I was the winner. I had viewed poker as organised fibbing ever since.

So really there were few less-deserving people of a trip to Vegas for the World Series of Poker. However, I was determined to at least put up a decent show in the tournament organised for the media because my haphazard approach would surely not work again. This was where Colin Wardley, a good poker player and friend, who was also on the trip, would come in useful.

Colin and I made for an odd pairing. Like me he was as thin as a rake but at 6ft 7in he towered above everything. So much so that when we were together I looked like his love-child from a failed affair with Sandi Toksvig. "Dad, dad," I would whine, pulling on his coat-tails. "Can we play poker now?" Colin re-acquainted me with the rules on the plane and we played a few games. I lost them all, although Colin admitted he had found it so easy because he could see the reflection of my cards in my spectacles. I wanted to play more but Colin was a difficult man to distract from what he considered was his calling in life: women. There was no question which of the three traps (birds, betting or booze) Colin would fall head first into, hurting himself terribly.

You knew he was about to impart what he thought were words of wisdom on the fairer sex when he would start a sentence with "I'm not being funny but…" And so it began in the short cab ride from the airport to our hotel on the Vegas strip.

"I'm not being funny but I don't think it would be optimistic to reckon we could get hold of at least four birds each," he said.

"I think that is the definition of optimism," I doubted.

"No, no, don't spoil it. Listen right, it's all about perception. One night we'll be Premiership footballers. These American sorts won't know the truth. I could be Liverpool striker Peter Crouch and you some young striker for Blackburn Rovers. Just make sure you shave. All about perception."

"Actually, I did have a phenomenal goalscoring record in schoolboy football…"

"There you go. Different story each night. Bankers the next, flashing the cash."

"If we had cash Colin, we'd already have birds clinging to our arms," I offered as we pulled up to the Treasure Island hotel.

"Point taken. See you by the pool to check out the talent."

It is an exhausting business watching bikini-clad girls strut by the pool in soaring temperatures, so after my first day in Vegas I was glad for a bed bigger than my flat (say what you like about Americans, they know how to furnish a hotel room) and woke refreshed for a day of exploring the casinos, eager to observe the habits of the American gambler.

Colin decided to spend another day at the pool. He had worked himself into a state late on day one, trying to work out what, and in which order, he would do to the members of Girls Aloud if he was locked away with them for a weekend. "Didn't sleep a wink, mate. I need to get this Girls Aloud schedule sorted to put my mind at rest. See yer later."

With the baking concrete poolside threatening to melt the sole of my flip-flops, I hotfooted it out of there with the Wynn hotel, the most prestigious of the Vegas complexes, and one of the finest in the world, my planned first stop. From there I fancied I would stroll to the Venetian to check out the interpretation of the Venice canals complete with gondolas, then to Paris to see the mini Eiffel Tower, hop over the road to the Bellagio with its famous fountains and on to Caesars Palace.

Emerging from Treasure Island my plan was quickly exposed as foolish and naïve. I had failed to account for the 40 degree heat, breathless air, which made walking arduous, and the sheer size of this city. The Strip is three miles long, which does not sound a lot, but the hotels and casinos are so vast that neighbouring complexes which look clustered and cosy on a map are virtually in different postcodes. And then there was getting to the other side of the road. I say road, I mean eight lanes of traffic. The Wynn was opposite Treasure Island but it took me half an hour to get there, navigating my way to a bridge in a panting, sweaty dishevelled mess to ensure that I stumbled into the Wynn lobby like John Mills out of *Ice-Cold in Alex*.

The excellent *Unofficial Guide to Las Vegas* describes the interior of the Wynn thus: "Matisse-inspired floral glass, mosaics swirl under your feet... rounding corridors, brightly beaded figurative folk art, tall sandstone Shivas... and shimmering Rajasthani textiles await." It all sounds very posh and could well be true. I couldn't say, though, as I was struggling to see through eyes half-blinded by the sweat cascading from my forehead and a frying-in-its-own-box brain which was struggling to process the images which were coming through.

What the *Unofficial Guide* does not tell you – and this is by no means surprising given that Americans are famed for their failure to grasp irony – is that Steve Wynn, the billionaire responsible for the hotel and, no overstatement this, Vegas as the gambling behemoth that it is today, suffers from retinitis pigmentosa, which affects his peripheral vision and his interaction with proximate objects. Therefore he is a great chap to play poker against although not in one of his casinos.

Wynn sounds a decent enough sort. Mainly because he

buys up all this terrific art – Picasso, Manet, Gauguin, Matisse, Vermeer and, er, Warhol (that'll be the old eyes again eh, Steve) – and then puts it on display in his hotels for people to come and gawp at. Previously his collection was on display at the Bellagio – which he built before flogging – and then moved it to the Wynn. Having recovered from my brief bout of heatstroke – I can at least confirm that the air conditioning is first class – I was keen to do a spot of chin scratching in front of some famous pieces. Not least *Le Rêve*, the Picasso portrait from which the resort was to take its name. Wynn eventually decided to go down the eponymous route because when showing off *Le Rêve* to some journalists, he struggled to interact with the proximate object and put his elbow through the canvas, writing off a cool $54 million from its value. If it was on display, it would be proof how money could not buy common sense.

"Excuse me, can you tell me where the gallery is?" I asked a Wynn worker.

"Sir, I'm so sad to inform you that the gallery closed sometime last year," came the reply with not a hint of insincerity.

That was a letdown. I trudged off hands in pockets, head bowed and into the casino, passing row after row of slot machines before arriving at the tables where I spotted a couple of faces I recognised, looking similarly glum as if they too had come to see Wynn's art collection. I was preparing to console them with the words "so you wanted to see the Vermeer as well, eh?" before realising that Frank Lampard and Shaun Wright-Phillips, the England footballers, probably thought that was some sort of expensive liquor. Besides they were wearing the scowl of Jesus in the temple because they were having a rum old time at a $5,000-a-hand blackjack table.

Learning from my earlier mistake, I jumped in a cab to continue my tour with the Venetian next on the list. It was not difficult to miss. The 1,000-guest-room tower loomed over a resort which is just the 200,000 square feet. The Venice canal was visible, too. From the cab window it looked impossibly tacky, like something the BBC would construct for a cash-short period drama. "Drive on," I said. "This looks a bit Gaudi," chuckling to myself at my inane art-based humour.

I was dropped at Flamingo, an old haunt for the gangsters, because I thought it would provide a nice contrast to the Wynn. If the Wynn mostly attracted Premier League footballers, Flamingo was for all sorts, like the south Californian surfer dudes who alongside me made their way across the grotty floor, dragging their knuckles behind them on their way to wiping out their wallets on craps. But really I could not tell the difference between the two casino halls. It was the same set-up. Rows of slots. Tables. More slots. A few more tables. Slots.

Surely there would be a noticeable change at Paris? But no. The four legs of the fake Eiffel Tower gatecrashed the main hall to give the feeling one was having a bet while major scaffolding was being put up. So another cab was hailed this time for the Bellagio, so grand it was used to film the *Ocean's Eleven* movie with one particularly memorable scene being Julia Roberts gliding (not literally, of course, they would have needed a stuntwoman for that) down a really splendid-looking staircase for her entrance. Inside I wandered around for what must have been half an hour trying to find, if you'll excuse me, Julia's entry point. But I could not. I didn't just walk around in one circle. I did several. I must have lapped one elderly couple at least twice and I'm sure security was beginning to track me, fearing some elaborate sting inspired by Julia and her gang. The problem was, and this point may be beginning to labour, that everything looked the same, similar, copied, cloned, lookalike, related etcetera. Caesars, which I hurried to in increasing desperation, was marginally better. A few Roman pillars dotted here and there broke up the monotony and the Pussycat Dolls lounge, which boasted unfeasibly attractive women as the croupiers (note to self: don't tell Colin) gave it something different.

Yet I was expecting more. I was sure that had I been blindfolded and placed in any of the casinos, I would struggle to make a stab at which one it was. It troubled me greatly. For I had arrived in Vegas pretty sure that people flocked here because they were able to gamble – not to be underestimated in a nation bordering on religious fundamentalism – and to do so in indelible surrounds. From what I had seen (okay, a small selection but let's not allow that to spoil it) I could not go home and say the casinos were mind blowing or anything near that. In short, I didn't get why Vegas was put on such a pedestal, not least because most people rejected the romantic table games but instead played the slot machines.

There are 200,000 of these in Vegas, offering a seat to those prepared to sit for hours with their mind in neutral, finger up their arse and their free digits cranking the handle of a console which rolls meaningless numbers in front of their eyes while playing a suicide-inducing tune which could have been composed by Bugs Bunny on crack. Then they order another bourbon from the waitress with tits straight from one of his cartoons. It made me cross. It certainly wasn't betting as I knew it; a titanic battle between punter and odds-setter to see who had the greater knowledge. There was no skill, no graft and sure as hell no element of courage unless you count the gin-soaked granny feeding her grandchildren's inheritance into a machine which lit up like a Catherine wheel every time she did so. These people did not equate with me, someone who spent hours poring over statistics, historical data and current trends in a bid to find an edge. That is what gambling and gamblers are about. Vegas, it seemed to me, is for the tomfool who arrives happy-go-lucky but often leaves hopelessly hooked, returning time after time with vain hope fuelled by the free booze and the bird with the big jugs that brings it, that he is one win, just one win, from being able to pack up for good.

Buoyed by the feeling that I was unlikely to be seduced by the betting, the booze or the birds on this trip I made my way back to Treasure Island for a spot of lunch at the ludicrously cheap buffet, which the casinos pride themselves on. The cheap 'all you can eat' variety, which, boy, is seen as a challenge and not an offer.

There were a tremendous amount of fat people around. Probably because Americans are tremendously fat. There were a couple of porkers in the queue ahead of me, called Dwayne and Darlene, who you could imagine appearing on *Oprah* or something in a few years, crying tears of lard about their terrible affliction.

"I'm so fat, I've got no self-respect." You ate it. Extra mayo. "I'm so fat, I don't have a boyfriend." You ate him. Extra cheese. "I'm so fat only my cat loves me." Supper.

Indeed if Americans could be as good at invading small countries as they were at eating then they would, er, rule the world. Dwayne and Darlene, both at least the size of a small country, and of the belief that Iran is something they once did for the ice-cream van, waddled into the buffet with the waitress posing this question: "Have you been here before?" Been before? Are you serious? They've never left. Their names are above the door. Their backsides have their own grooves in the seats.

The feeding process at the buffet made for fascinating viewing. A bride, still in her dress after being married in the chapel in the hotel, scooped spare ribs on to her plate, another weighty individual sat down with a trough piled high with artery-busting fare and then ordered a diet coke, while everyone ignored the dusty old relic of a sign at the 40-option dessert counter, which read hopefully "ask about our sugar-free desserts".

This was all just one cycle in the brilliantly-designed Vegas ecosystem. Nonetheless it was probably the most important. The aim of the house is, firstly, to get people gambling and secondly, that they don't do it anywhere else. If they fail, the casino closes. So other than offer the standard array of gambling options, they throw in dirt-cheap fattening food, comfort food if you will, to make gamblers feel better after a big loss. And if you really want to be cynical, and I don't see any reason why we shouldn't, the casinos would much rather cater for the fatsos (for a start their self-esteem is lower, a common trait of gamblers) because if a podger was to attempt to leave a casino to brave the sweltering heat outside, they would stand much more of a chance of their fat starting to cook, being stretchered back into the cooling air of the gambling hall and cursing their foolishness for thinking there was anything better for them to do than say, a thin person. So feed 'em up.

This master plan coupled with the free drink and in-house entertainment – for example Treasure Island hosted a Cirque de Soleil show – makes it all the harder to resist the cheeky punt here and there. Why bother with a journey to see what the other casinos have to offer? And just in case it works so well that people are still gambling in the wee hours, there are no clocks to even tell them it is getting late, no signposts to direct them back to their rooms and, get this, pure oxygen is pumped in to keep everyone bright as a button so you won't get tired in the first place. Hell, Caesars even put the face of hooked-nose crooner Celine Dion on their chips. And who would not want to give them back? Clever stuff.

Feeling extremely pleased that I had cracked the Vegas lark, I went off to re-join Colin by the pool. He was easily spotted. Towering over the bar, his white legs – two days of almost continual sun worshipping had not altered his pasty complexion – looked like a pair of goalposts. "What are those two pieces of string hanging down from your shorts, Colin?" I asked on approach.

"What? Eh?" he said as he checked his garments, fearing a terrible fashion faux pas which had hindered his success with the ladies.

"Oh, sorry, they're your legs," I told him.

"Never mind that, I'm at a critical stage here. See that blonde bird dangling her legs over the side of the pool? There. At the far end."

"Yep. She's stunning."

"I'm not being funny but she's been giving me the eye all day. It's been a bit embarrassing, actually."

Well aware that staring at anything even remotely unusual – and Colin was as much of a draw as the Eiffel Tower or Sphinx if you ask me – is the wont of folk in these parts, I attempted to put him off taking matters farther: "To be honest, she's really, really attractive and probably out of your league so let's just have a drink and forget it."

"Oh that's brilliant that is," he retorted. "Knock my confidence why don't you? I told you, it's all about perception."

"But you've been here on your own all day. What do you think she'll perceive from that?"

"You're doing it again!"

"I'm just trying to save you a rejection. Go over there if you want."

"I'm going to. Watch and learn."

So off Colin stalked towards the pool, the flashing reflection off his ivory beanpoles causing several pool-goers to shield their eyes as if someone was tormenting them with a mirror. The girl sat serenely by the edge, dangling her legs in the water and making mini whirlpools with her dainty feet. Colin, stirred by this vision of loveliness, lengthened his stride, eating up the distance between him and his intended target. His pace was quick, meaning he was steaming towards a small boy in armbands and swimming goggles, a dangerous hazard for those of us with even the most customary of gaits. But he spotted him, effected a dazzling shimmy and turned briefly toward me to purse his lips together and let out a small but triumphant "phew!". This meant he did not see the line of sun loungers which he had drifted off course towards during celebration. Smack! His shins struck the plastic of one with enough force to double him up in pain. "Fuck!" he cried. She was definitely looking at him now. Still bending down he rested his hands on the lounger, only for it to give way and, with perfect timing as his shoulders sloped and his backside rose further to the heavens, its legs caught on the concrete floor, the friction permitting a ripping flatulent sound. "Oh Jesus," Colin whimpered. Everyone was looking at him now.

Thousands from all over the world qualified to play in the World Series of Poker by logging on to the net in the wee hours, probably wearing just their pants. It proved to be a good warm-up. With the local weather station reporting in the morning it was to be the hottest day in Nevada's history, a sweltering 117°F, the hopefuls could have been forgiven for turning up at the Rio All-Suite Hotel and Casino, the venue for the tournament, in just their undergarments.

Those that did not qualify online paid $10,000 to play alongside Chris Moneymaker, Joe Hachem and Isabelle Mercier, some of the most famous names in the game. That was if they could hand over the cash. Organisers had told prospective players that the fee could be paid by credit card before changing their minds. It was the first bluff of the eight-day event. The result was angry and red-faced gamblers looking to beg, borrow or steal as Colin and I walked into the lobby. Mind you there was not a shortage of money around. Hollywood superstars Ben Affleck, Matt Damon and Adam Sandler were on hand to play in a charity game to raise funds for the crisis in Darfur. I reckoned that if they managed to play better than they acted all their winnings should go straight to fundraiser Ante Up For Africa. Affleck, with the way his career was going, may have been tempted to buy into the main event himself. With in excess of $12m going to the winner, Affleck's wooden and detached style fitted perfectly for poker. And the pot was probably about $2m more than what he earned per movie. Ooh, hark at me criticising someone's 'style'. I was only here just to watch and attempt to learn, of course, and was in no real position to disparage any of the players brave enough to get involved in the big action.

Whatever happens in the Main Event, as it is called despite it being effectively the world championship, you can be sure of two things; the sport will find new stars from the competitors. But the rest will leave minus the shirt on their back – which was not such a bad thing in the heat – returning to their corner of the globe, logging on to the computer and shutting out the rest of society, apart from mum when she brings up some meatloaf.

This is the thing about poker. Were it not for the geek who sits in his room all day, logged on and alternating between the two different sorts of shuffling, the game would have died out years ago. Before the millennium some casinos were even closing their poker rooms but these days players online have increased by 2,000 per cent and the market is worth close to an astounding $2 billion. And the cream of the nerdy crop are handsomely rewarded. Remember at school that spotty kid with thick-rimmed glasses, trousers constantly hitched up as if he feared the classroom would flood at any second and who walked around with a sore butt by order of the sign stuck to his back that said 'kick me'? You know, the one who was capable of reciting bus timetables for Greater Manchester in the 1970s. Well, he's one of the world's best poker players now. A hero to millions of his boffin, boss-eyed-from-too-much-shuffling brethren. Pictured with Miss World contestants after winning a tournament worth sums which only he could configure. As Colin would say: "it's all about perception", but it is still very annoying.

As far as I could make out, having a brain like one of those expensive calculators – has anyone ever worked out what that button does which looks like a tick? Open a portal to another world? Let the cat out? – was key. So too insomnia. I was sure sleeplessness could be the most important trait in deciding who walked away with the big bucks.

Just to get through the first round, a player would have to remain alert for a whopping 12 hours – that's three hours longer than it took to fly to Vegas from Gatwick. And you don't have the option of watching some awful movie 'starring' Chris Rock. Well you could I suppose, but it wouldn't do your chances much good. And if it's boring to play in as I overheard one player suggest – "would it be terribly wrong to fall asleep at the table" – it's even worse to watch. When you've seen one card game, you've seen them all – even if there are more than 150 of them to choose from. It should be exciting when you consider that the chip leader when I was doing my scouting mission had built an impenetrable-looking wall of chips worth $107,000. But it wasn't.

What we needed, I thought, was a player to fall foul of the swearing rule, which is far from dull, I can tell you. This has caused terrific controversy in the poker community. In 2006 it was forbidden for a player to use the word 'fuck' in any context. And if one did, they were told to leave their seat at the table for a 20-minute cooling-off period.

It had been modified slightly this year after one player challenged it after being ejected for using a profanity in a punchline with the immortal words to a tournament official: "I think it's a terrible rule... you c***." Now you have to swear at a fellow player in an aggressive manner to take a walk. See the former sentence for a clue as to how to do that. It's not a bad ploy if you're beginning to feel tiredness kicking in or just a general feeling of being piqued about a game with such a slim chance of reward. Take Dennis Frederick for example. He hit a royal flush holding Qd Jd on a board of Kd 10s 6d Ad 10d. I know this because it was in the newsletter which was handed around. And his prize for the first royal flush of the tournament? A free 40-minute massage. What his response was to such a measly reward for such a fine feat was not recorded. "Is that fucking it?" hopefully.

Still, it is serious business this poker. And you know it is something special when you spot the queues for the toilets are 20 deep and the normally-packed buffet hall is bare. Anything that can stop Americans eating must be worth it. And of course it is. The stakes are high enough for most to consider not waddling in for firsts, let alone seconds. I bet Dwayne and Darlene don't play poker. Indeed if the US government ever decided to get serious about solving the nation's obesity problem, all they need do is to stage a big bucks tournament in each state, each month and make it compulsory for the local Weight Watchers group to attend. The weight would drop off. After all, Amarillo Slim wasn't called Amarillo Fat was he?

Inside the game hall the players take their seats after a break and sip cautiously from water as they wait for the announcer, in the style of the best boxing announcers, to declare "Dea-lers! Shuffle! Your! Cards!" I must admit it was a rather impressive sight in that small snapshot of time and I felt slightly anxious as to how I would cope when sitting down to play in just a few hours' time.

There was still no sign of any eating as play began to the constant pitter-patter of chips being passed nervously from one hand to the other. Close your eyes and you would think you were in a field full of crickets. To play with your stake is the easiest way for coping with the tension it seemed. Others listen to MP3 players, get a massage while in their game seat or bring along lucky mascots. Yes, grown men from rough and tumble places like Michigan or Pittsburgh actually bring a cuddly toy with them. "My wife gave it to me," said Floyd, clutching a small, pink rabbit toy. "I get a ribbing for it but, hell, I'm real superstitious and I wouldn't play without it."

"Has it got a name?" I ask.

"Er, no, no. I just like to have it with me," said Floyd unconvincingly. I didn't believe him, I bet he called it Flopsy and cuddled up to it at night.

Now and again the constant shrill of the crickets was broken by a call of "all in on table…" followed shortly after by a groan and the sight of a man with his head in his hands leaving the arena. To have paid $10,000 to enter a tournament and go out only a few hours in must be difficult to swallow. But at least they could console themselves by going to the buffet and stuffing their faces.

I had no such qualms about eating before my big moment. PokerStars, the company hosting the media tournament, had kindly laid on a rather super buffet. I was just tucking into a trifle when players from the PokerStars stable filed into the room. There had been a promise made that we would be able to pick the brains of these 'super stars' before play began, so reluctantly I put down my spoon and cornered Isabelle Mercier, a French Canadian, who has caused a bit of a stir in the poker world because of her striking looks and an aggressive style which has earned her the nickname No Mercy. Unsurprisingly Colin made a beeline for an attractive Dutch blonde.

Mercier started with $10,000 in her pocket and played in tournaments seven hours a day to rise to become one of the most famous pros in the world. The reason was a word which crops up often in poker circles: 'aggression'. She was very keen to get across that I should be the intimidator rather than the intimidated in a tournament which would include legends like Joe Hachem, Greg Raymer and Chris Moneymaker. Fat chance.

"Aggression is very important. It's a key element so don't be meek in what you do."

"So should I be snarling at people?" I asked.

"I don't think so," she said. "That doesn't look your style. Some people choose to barely move or speak and that is a form of aggression."

I wondered whether her preoccupation with hostility was because she was a woman trying to make her way in a man's world. Mistake. She got a bit, well, aggressive.

"I don't like that question," she bristled. "I must have been asked that 500 times. What difference does it make that I'm a woman? We're not playing football or sprinting. I'm not from another planet." She was right of course and I was not about to argue, even if it would have been good preparation.

So aggression at the poker table meant, as far as I could make out, raising or calling out of line with your actual chance of winning. Why this was a good ploy escaped me but who was I to argue with advice from people who had won lots doing it? Rather disappointingly it did not mean questioning the parentage of my fellow players or jabbing my finger into their chests, although I found it hard not to consider the latter when I discovered that Shannon Elizabeth would be on my table. For those of you who do not know Elizabeth, she was the actress who played the eye-wateringly alluring Nadia in the 1999 comedy *American Pie*. This was a potentially damaging development. I mean, how on earth would Colin cope given his poolside disaster and his information that the Dutch girl was "up 'er own arse"? In an effort to discover an aggressive streak, and whet the whistle for some smooth-talk on Elizabeth, Colin and I made use of the complimentary bar for a couple of hours before attending the pre-tournament press conference. Mistake. While each of the PokerStars players were being announced to the media in that very American way, Colin and I swayed and squinted, finally slurring in unison "I'm not being funny, but Shannon Elizabeth keeps looking at me."

Elizabeth wasn't looking at either of us. I knew that because when she sat down between us at the game table she did not so much as glance at the two inebriated Englishmen contorting their faces into attempted snarls, merely succeeding in looking as if they had just suffered massive, massive strokes.

A stroke victim would have probably been able to focus better. I could not keep my pie-eyes off Elizabeth. The last time I had been this close to her was when my nose was pressed to a television screen and she was taking off her clothes. She was similarly out of focus then come to think of it.

'Grr, I'm a tiger! I'm a tiger!' I told myself as I was dealt a pair of sevens in the first hand, throwing in half of my stake. "What are you doing?" demanded Colin, who somehow seemed to be holding it together much better than me. "That was a shit bit of play." Hands two and three passed with minimal damage and I folded straight away in the fourth simply because I had no idea whether I had a couple of aces as I was too busy looking at Elizabeth's fine pair. In hand five, however, everything was set up to go my way. I was feeling nicely aggressive, if that isn't a contradiction, after recovering from my early embarrassment and had been dealt a pair of kings. Even I knew that was a reasonable hand. So, remembering Mercier's words I went 'all-in'. In other words, chucking every chip forth in a shoulder-punching show of bravado. Feeling very pleased with myself and the large pot I was about to win, I gave Elizabeth a wink and Colin, who looked at me as if I was deranged, a knowing look. When a third king arrived as a community card, I almost scoffed at the ease with which I was putting supposedly more knowledgeable players in the shade. There they were, nervously passing chips from one hand to the other, recreating the noise I had heard earlier of the anxious crickets infesting a country field. I was in the next field along, gloriously sunning myself in the summer haze, chewing on some straw with a pint of cider, safe in the knowledge that I knew I was soon to be making hay. Mistake. You can imagine that it came as a ghastly shock to discover that I had read my cards horribly and catastrophically wrong. Somehow one of the kings I thought I had had morphed into a jack and the other a queen. "Thought I had a pair of kings," I mumbled to Elizabeth. "See yer later."

The betting, the booze, the birds. Las Vegas gets you in the end.

Chapter 12

Emotion – New Orleans

When it comes to betting, heart should never rule head. It is the golden rule; a comfort rug to be guarded from the seam-picking grasp of the boney, long-fingered, money-grabbing bookies. Unsurprising then that most punters discard it at the door of the betting shop. For if they were to wrap themselves tightly in its cosseting fibres, bookmakers would, eventually, go out of business. They remain all-powerful because bettors fritter away cash on emotional punts, failing to grasp that although it would be a "wonderful story" for the golfer who is playing in his first tournament since returning from a serious illness to triumph, it would not be a wonderful bet. Or backing the cricketer playing in his final Test to score a century because there "won't be a dry eye in the house". Sniff, sniff. Not a dry eye in the house. Your house. Your wife. When she discovers you've gambled the month's shopping budget and leaves you. Far too often punters allow their misty eyes to obscure rational thought processes, cloud unbreakable facts and warp the odds staring back at them from the bookmakers' coupon.

That's not to say it's not easy to come over all dewy-eyed. There are few examples in black and white to provide encouragement. Save from the Bible, which, let's face it, you can interpret any which way to support an argument. Good old Jesus H Christ – the H did not stand for Holy as some claim, but in fact High-stakin', a gambling moniker like Amarillo Slim or Nick the

Greek – loved a cheeky punt. What? You didn't know JC was a gambler? Sure, he was like, y'know, *so* into punting. And one of the most successful at enveloping himself in that comfort rug, although back then it was just loincloth. Who could forget his astounding show of emotional discipline when the Devil asked him to turn water into wine, a 4-1 shot at the time according to a bookie chum who very kindly priced up the market especially for this book*. Despite being well capable of landing those odds and with emotions running high, he kept his discipline, gripped that loincloth just that bit tighter, and declined. Why?

Because he knew the value was still to come. Returning from the dead was a fancier trick and one with much bigger odds (probably 1,000-1 according to my stingy pal), which would most certainly have been slashed had he taken on Satan with the vino wager. He died for all our sins – wasting money on England in major football tournaments, staking on the manager we want to take over at our favourite football team and backing that well-known jockey to win on his last ride.

The only person I knew who showed Jesus-like discipline for rejecting emotion was a sub-editor on one of my first newspapers. He was a gambling fiend. In fact, his attitude bordered on the callous. Colleagues would test his legendary status by asking him whether he would attend the funeral of his desk buddy, who he had sat side by side with for the last 15 years, when he died. "Nah," would come the reply. "There'll be racing on." Or question him whether he would bludgeon a swan with his bare hands if it would guarantee a cup final ticket. "I'd do it for a third-round one."

I once watched him with amazement when, stooped over his desk watching greyhound racing on television and chomping his fingernails, as was his wont when he had a bet on, he barely looked up from the screen during a heart-rupturing tale from the previously mentioned desk buddy about an acquaintance who had found out his pregnant wife had cancer, and they would have to abort the child. At the end of the story, he pointed to the screen and grunted: "See this dog 'ere, I've had a monkey on that and it's got done by a nose on the line."

*When I asked for these odds, my bookmaker acquaintance made me chuckle. "The wine trick would not have been too surprising because it was not his first miracle, so there was form for that," he said. "It was a bit Paul Daniels, too. Coming back from the dead? Well, that's the biggy. No-one would've thought that possible."

Despite that loss-making incident, he was a hugely successful gambler. It was his attitude I would need to replicate to crack this betting lark. Detaching the heart strings so I could not be pulled in the wrong direction was necessary surgery. So cockfighting, which, crucially, was illegal to gamble on – and involved unnecessary pain to God's creatures – in New Orleans, the murder capital of the US, it had to be. It was clear the right decision had been made as soon as I began telling friends of my desire to travel to bet on a sport which was deemed cruel enough to be banned everywhere else in America. There is nothing quite like the certain death of animals to stir ire. "You should be ashamed of yourself" and "you'll get butt-raped" were the regular responses. I was perturbed by both. Which is exactly how I wanted to feel. It was going to be brutal, I told myself. Cock-a-doodle-don't say I didn't warn you.

Disappointment. That was the overriding emotion when I arrived in New Orleans. I didn't see anyone get mugged, shot, or for that matter, 'butt-raped'. Nor did I spot anyone who looked like they might be capable of such crimes. Come on, this was supposed to be America's badlands for goodness sake; a city so ghastly that it had a murder rate of 70 per 100,000. To put that into context, New Orleans' Superdome had a capacity of 80,000. Imagine it full and then come to terms with the absolute fact that 56 poor souls in that crowd would end up victims of homicide. It is a city so evil that in 2005 when Hurricane Katrina blew in and displaced a large wedge of residents to Houston, Texas, the murder rate there soared by 25 per cent. These were bad people. Yet everyone I came across was absolutely charming.

This may have been because I was housed in the French Quarter, the main tourist destination, and that most crimes were concentrated in low-income neighbourhoods, such as housing projects, that are sites of open-air drug trade. It really wouldn't do at all. I was briefly cheered when I noticed that my hotel backed on to Bourbon Street, world-famous for debauchery levels which could make those of the loosest morals sit down and have a good hard think. It was pleasant enough, however. Its narrow streets were illuminated by the neon lights of bars either side to stroll down; it was like walking through the middle of a rainbow. There was no sign of any crack whores – are they something to do with drugs or just hookers who are *really* good at their jobs, like a crack sniper? – and even the titty bars seemed rather tame. One offered you the chance to 'wash the girl of your choice', odd because I was sure that the people who frequented such places were after a more dirty experience. Another boasted of 'love acts'. Even I was not green enough to believe that whatever the 'models' got up to in there was remotely close to amour.

Walking back to my hotel to rest my head, I was concerned that I had not seen any sign that my emotional resolve would be tested. A reminder to be patient greeted me when I turned off Bourbon and on to New Orleans Street. At the end of it was St Louis Cathedral. On its cream-coloured frontage was a huge dark shadow of old High-stakin', Jesus Christ himself. In the cathedral's gardens a five-foot statue of the big guy had been lit from the front so that when night fell he rose up tenfold to cover the wall behind in menacing fashion, with arms outstretched as if to make a plea to those below indulging in a multitude of sins. The blue skies and bright sunshine which welcomed my second day in New Orleans did little to convince me the emotive tide would turn, especially when I strolled past the cathedral to notice High-stakin' had retreated to his smaller form. I kept walking, through the pretty palm-tree potted Jackson Square where Old Glory hung limp above a statue of General Andrew Jackson on his steed declaring "the union must and shall be preserved!"and to my first sight of the meandering charm of the great Mississippi. I sat on its bank and watched its brown water jostling along the course of what, depending on which encyclopedia you believe, is the third or fourth largest river in the world. A three-way tussle for ear superiority was underway between the strains of street jazz, a steamboat's pipes playing Dean Martin's 'That's Amore' and the constant pinking of the trams behind. It was idyllic. Particularly when the steamboat decided it was time to transport me back to the days of Mark Twain and set off for its hourly trip. It further churned up the murky waters with a red wheel big enough to keep the world's population of hamsters in peak physical condition and blasted its horn to give it a resounding victory in the musical stakes, much to the delight of its delirious passengers.

Believe me when I say that there is something very odd that happens to a man when he steps on to a boat: he turns into an utter moron. As soon as it leaves dock, he will become a gibbering half-wit in awe at his ability to conquer water. His grin will be huge so his teeth protrude to the extent you could uncap beer bottles on them and he will point at everything and nothing on the shoreline, as if he has never before seen a warehouse, jetty or inlet. Worse, he will wave. And he will wave at everyone, occasionally accompanied by a 'yoo-hoo!' Those on the banks meekly wave back, despite knowing they are too far away from this lunatic to be identified in any way and thus be forced to become friends forever. Out of embarrassment they raise a hand to acknowledge the waterborne nuisance and so condone his thought process: 'Look at me! I'm on a boat, I'm better than you. My wife's prettier. I have a bigger penis.' Do not doubt the arrogance stretches this far. In fact, I would say the act of one stepping aboard boats, are to blame for much misery. History is littered with examples of how everything was calm, plain sailing if you like, and then someone got on a boat. The British Empire only started because a couple of chaps went out for a row, got lost, saw a small country and thought 'right, we'll have that'. The consequences of Mr and Mrs Hitler's decision to take their son to the Austrian lakes for a mini-break are still being felt. Granted the seeds of tyranny may well have been planted in Adolf's mind before he set foot on 'Das Boot' but boating just brought it out of him. On a wider scale, look at people who list 'yachting' as a hobby. All wankers.

"You're all gonna fucking drown! Ha! Ha!" That is what I wish I could have shouted. I like to think I would have done had it not first come from the mouth of a drunk, shuffling towards me, swigging and spilling a bottle of cheap bourbon to bring a cliché to life.

"You know why they're so happy don'tcha?" said the drunk.

"Er, no, no I don't," I answered.

"It's 'cos a third of the US population take three pills or more a day for ailments which the pharmaceutical companies tell them they have."

Well, this was the most lucid and potentially intelligent drunk I had ever encountered. "Interesting," I countered. "Got any more?"

"This river isn't the life force it used to be," he said, pointing at the one-mile Gulf of Mississippi between this bank and the other. "The antecedent of nature has been accelerated by the interference of man. The water's too oxygenated." I don't think that made sense but it sounded bloody good. "The Cold War only ended because we paid off the Russians with billions of dollars." Okay, two out of three wasn't bad.

"I like you, Pete," he offered – I don't know where he got Pete from – "you're a hustler."

Now the dictionary defines a hustler firstly as, 'an enterprising person determined to succeed' and secondly as 'an expert gambler who seeks out challenges'. I couldn't say I was unhappy with either, although there had to be strong doubts over the legitimacy of this man's character judgement considering he had guessed my name, was drinking from a very cheap-looking bottle of liquor and had his shoes on the wrong feet. Apart from that he was well presented in khaki trousers and a blue polo shirt, untucked. He had that greyish stubble that all drunks seem to have, straighter and stronger as if the booze had hair growth boosting properties and as he leaned over, somewhat shakily, to speak I noticed a scar on his forehead. "I'm Sean Kamplinski, originally from Boston, been here ten years."

"Ah, Boston," I said. "You know their basketball team are in town to play the New Orleans Hornets don't you?"

"No way! They're my team, man. Oh, they'll win for sure, for sure."

"Really? I read in the paper that the Hornets are doing really well at the moment…"

"Ha!", interrupted Kamplinski. "You're hustling me! Man, I knew you were a hustler! I bet you five bucks the Celtics win. Just like everything in this town, the Hornets have gone to sheeeet." He said the word "sheeeet" with particular venom.

Of course I wasn't hustling him, merely making conversation. Indeed if there was one section of society that I didn't want to be betting against, it was the destitute. I would imagine they have problems paying. Still it was only five bucks and if I won, taking money from someone who had fallen on hard times was harsh in the extreme. My sub-editing pal would be extremely proud.

"Okay," I said. "But how will I find you when I want to collect my winnings?"

"For a start there won't be no winnings," slurred Kamplinski. "But I'll be right here. Always here in the mornin'. Been coming here for years, Pete."

"Can we just clear something up, given we've had a wager and all, that my name isn't Pete, it's Ed."

"Sure, sure, sure it is. I like you, you're a hustler. An English hustler. Ha!"

There comes a time when you chat to someone like Kamplinski

that they tell you their 'story'. The tale of woe which has seen them fall from grace into a horrible hole. It is as inevitable as two English people, who don't like each other that much, meeting unexpectedly and talking about the weather.

Pre-empting Kamplinski and alerting the tear ducts to standby, I asked: "Where did you get the scar?"

"Katrina gave me this," he said pointing to the wound. "When she blew I lost my possessions, my home, my girlfriend. So I started sleeping under the interstate at Claiborne and one night I got busted up by some other guys who said it was their spot. So I went into shelter. Got a heroin addiction, too."

Not quite sure what to say to that, I offered, uselessly, "well, I suppose it is very, er, addictive." He looked at me awkwardly. "But you're very matter of fact about it?"

"Gotta be, man. Besides I'm off the drugs — been off it for about two weeks, which is why I'm on the booze," he said, casting a forlorn look at the liquor bottle. "But I ain't sorry. Best way to be the way this town is going."

"What's wrong with it?" I asked.

"How long have you got? Katrina destroyed all the drug centres who help people like me. And they sure aren't rebuilding 'em. Without that kinda help you can't get a full-time job. Without a full-time job you can't get your home back. The rent on my place doubled after Katrina. At least I'm trying to get clean but those thousands sleeping underneath the interstate have nothing. Apart from crime."

I found such a statement of clarity surprising from a man who clearly went through life in a haze, although again he spoiled it soon after by insisting that the Salvation Army had "stolen" $20m of Katrina aid. Still, finding out more about the effects of the hurricane seemed necessary. "Hell, they run tours of the worst-hit areas," offered Kamplinski. "Just further down the promenade there. Anything for a buck in this town." So I bade farewell to Kamplinski, promising to find him again when our basketball bet had been settled. "You stay safe, Pete," he shouted after me. "I'll stay off the drugs, man… gonna stay off it!"

Further up the prom was a small hut with a sign saying 'Katrina Tour – America's Worst Disaster!'. If that sounded boastful, fear not. The lady dispensing tickets greeted me with anything but brio insofar as I pondered whether the plastic panel separating us was not to keep me from getting at her, rather the other way around. Her manner was understandable. Her workplace was cramped. And she cramped her workplace as she conformed to the stereotypical American fatty. Bless her, she had found room for a microwave and it was possible that if she continued to balloon at that rate we could witness the first human Play-do Fun Factory, with her oozing out of every crack and cranny of the kiosk.

On the bus I was greeted by a cheery smile from our guide, Sandi, who in the tradition of all coach drivers – it must be in the manual – had at hand a bucket. Normally such a receptacle is there for passengers who are overexcited, travel sick or drunk. My fellow tourists looked old enough and wise enough to be none of those, so it had to be there for collecting donations for Katrina victims. Barely had the engine started when Sandi started to tighten the emotional strings. "We used to have such a bubbly attitude to life before the levees broke, now reality has taken over." Of course it was all very sad. The problem was that Sandi spoke with such a wonderful Louisiana purr – smacking her lips at the end of every sentence as if she had just devoured a slice of cake – that she could have told you your house had just been washed away, and it would have softened the blow. At some stage during the hurricane she probably did exactly that. The loss of homes was a reality for thousands – 12,000 people in the Big Easy were homeless – who had relied on the government and Army Corps of Engineers to keep them safe in the city, half of which was below sea level. The failure was a fine example of academics convincing themselves of things supposedly less intelligent people could not. They did not reckon that the erosion of 1.9 million acres of wetlands for oil and gas pipelines would make

New Orleans vulnerable, despite such land acting as a sponge when a tidal surge, a consequence of a hurricane, rushed in. For every four miles of marsh or swamp that a surge crosses, one foot is absorbed. Nor did they believe the levees, which had been found to be brittle as long ago as 1986, needed reinforcing.

Twenty or so minutes after leaving the riverside we were to the east of the city, which was hardest hit. We passed the St Rita nursing home in St Bernard parish where 35 residents drowned, countless wrecked homes with the infamous 'graffiti' crosses to signify how many dead people were found inside and sometimes just porches, where houses used to be, for a whole neighbourhood. There were houses with holes smashed in the roof because their owners had gone to the attic to escape the flood water, only for it to keep rising. They were lucky. There were houses which were razed because people had been advised to switch off the electric and light candles, unaware that the water had skewed gas pipes, causing leaks. When they struck a match they blew themselves to Kingdom Come.

Sandi turned the screw some more. "Just here," she said, pointing to another skeletal home, "I found a boy with beautiful braids in his hair. He kept asking me 'what shall I do, what shall I do?' I asked him what he meant. 'I've got nothing. The robbers took everything. My daddy told me to run. Then they shot my daddy in the face.'"

At this point I longed for a portable television showing greyhound races so I could turn to the person sat to my right and say "see this dog 'ere, I've had a monkey on that and it's got done by a nose on the line." Anything to be distracted from the scenes of desolation or the shocking stories. I had wanted a sentimental examination, and boy was I getting it. Thankfully, Sandi, like some modern-day Shakespeare, followed the misery with mirth. We passed a house which had the slogan 'Kev and Mandy are ok!' spray painted on it. "They're not," she said. "They got divorced." It was much-needed light relief. This was three years on from Katrina and it was evident that New Orleans remained in an awful state. Whether that was the fault of the Bush administration, the much-maligned Federal Emergency Management Agency (FEMA) or, tenuously, the Salvation Army for pinching all the cash as Kamplinski spouted, I didn't know. But I was sure of one thing: Sandi was going to need a bigger bucket.

Later that evening in my hotel room, I watched the result of the Hornets versus Celtics match come in, in between countless adverts from pharmaceutical companies pushing their new super drug with the voiceover artist sounding as if he had just downed a bottle of whatever pills they were selling. "New! Choke-croak! Kills! Asthma! Dead!" And then in a softer tone on the come down. "Choke-croak should not be taken by people with chronic respiratory problems. May cause vomiting, diarrhoea, palpitations, heart attack and asthma." Good old Kamplinski was right about the pharmaceuticals but not the basketball. The Hornets emerged victorious. Not that that was going to improve my mood. The Katrina tour had been upsetting and, I apologise for sounding a bit of a wimp here, I was beginning to feel a little anxious, fragile even. Tomorrow I would drive the four hours to Toomey, a town on the edge of the state line with Texas, to bet on birds ripping each other to pieces. Even worse, there was the prospect of a visit to the animal rights people beforehand.

I was up at an early hour to take a cab back to the airport to hire a car for my trip to the cockfight and was surprised to bump in to Kamplinski as I waited for my ride.

"How you doing?" I asked as he walked past on the way to his riverside seat.

"I'm still off it, Pete!"

Of course, I should have asked him for my money but was distracted; feeling uneasy about what could potentially lay in store. I was going deep into the south and japes about 'butt-rape' were making a prolonged bid to dominate my conscience. My brain was slightly out of sync with what was happening, a symptom of early rising. When I arrived at the airport I did not understand a word that the car rental woman told me.

For all I knew I could have bought the car for the amount of forms I signed. And goodness knows how much gas I bought. She offered me half a dozen different pricing options which seemed to be roughly based on questions an American kid would get at high school maths. "If Cletus needs to hire a car in order to travel from the Bayou to town in order to give Betty-Sue a damned good whuppin' cos she said 'Freebird' is better than 'Sweet Home Alabama', and the only vehicle he can get does 42 to the gallon, how many bottles of Bud will he consume before he decides he is in a fit state to drive?" I just said yes to all of them, received a puzzled look in return and handed over the credit card.

Very kindly the lady walked me to my purchase, which was just as well because the 100 cars in the parking lot looked identical. She handed me the key and paperwork, voluminous enough to be recycled for a national newspaper run, and I was on my way. Although I wasn't. The key would not go into the ignition. I ratcheted this way and that, softly at first and then more aggressively while making that 'urrrgggggh' noise that people reserve for tasks which are not actually strenuous, like opening a stubborn jar of jam, and rocking back and forth in my seat for leverage. Wary that I might be having some sort of fit, the car rental lady shouted "are you okay?"

"No!" I replied. "I can't make it go," continually trying to force the key while pushing all manner of buttons, pulling levers, switching the in-car light on and off and looking generally panicked. With my friend tapping on the window whining "Come out! Come out! Come out!", if Richard O'Brien had turned up with a mouth organ it would have been exactly like an episode of *The Crystal Maze*. "You're using the wrong key," said the car rental lady. "That is for the gas cap."

It was an inauspicious start to my four-hour drive to the Texas border, which was to be broken up by a visit to the Louisiana Society for the Prevention of Cruelty to Animals. I know you're thinking 'why do you want to visit those do-gooders?' but one of the annoying traits inbuilt in journalists is to discover both sides of the story. This will hardly be a newsflash for you but the LSPCA were very much on a different side to the cockfighters. If I was going to talk to cockfighters about their sport, it seemed only fair that I should have a natter with the people that had successfully got it banned. I suppose now would be a pertinent time to fill you in, friend, of how Louisiana had belatedly become the last US state to ban cockfighting.

Central to it all was gambling. Unnecessary suffering to animals tends to make the blood bubble of the animal rights sorts. Throw in anguish and distress for the pleasure of people making money out of it and they get decidedly uppity. So the LSPCA wanted legislation to get banned a practice where specially-bred birds with razor blades of up to four inches attached to their legs fought to the death. Their real bone of contention, however, was the claim that birds were worked into a frenzy to fight while spectators were in a similar lather, baying for blood and bucks.

The cockfighters, or to give them their proper title, the Louisiana Gamefowl Breeders' Association, argued that in a state where there was a rich blend of cultures from Cajun French to Creole, cockfighting was part of its unique heritage. There were also noises about it being traditional. This point was despatched with ease. Just because something was done hundreds of years ago didn't make it right. Slavery, women being denied the vote and Bruce Forsyth were all popular once, you know. In July 2007 state legislation was passed making it illegal to gamble on cockfighting and in August 2008 – the third anniversary of Katrina incidentally – the sport would be banned in Louisiana completely.

As I sat in the car park of the LSPCA shelter, of warehouse-style construction and painted bright blue, I would like to say that I was deliberating thoughtfully about the respective arguments. No. Instead my mind was preoccupied with the name of LSPCA chief executive, Ana Zorrilla, which seemed an anagram-lover's dream – all I could come up with was 'anal czar ore oil' and that was cheating in a way because I added her job title letters CEO – and preconceptions about her ilk.

For a long while I had 'issues' with animal rights people, something which was spawned by my mother forcing me to go to country craft fairs as a youngster. "You can't go racing with Dad all the time." As far as I was concerned, craft fair attendees, eco warriors and animal lovers were the same. If they weren't trying to sell you things they'd made, they'd be droning on about the polar ice caps and how dogs and cats should be given the vote. What binds the three together is wicker. They love it. It's almost a currency in the circles they move in. If they're not carrying around their hare-brained ideas in specially fashioned wicker baskets, they're wearing waistcoats made out of the stuff. A moment's loss of concentration when chatting to Zorrilla could result in her fitting me with a three-piece wicker suit or ordering a solar panel for the house.

There were plenty of do-gooder types in the car park, which was kept in pristine order. Manicured lawns and tree bark sprinkled all over as if soil was unsightly. There was an affluent-looking mom and dad who had brought their two Nazi-blond kids to the shelter to pick up a rescued golden retriever and they were showering it with affection, wearing *Brady Bunch* smiles and shoes which looked suspiciously like cardboard. Can I get one more anagram? 'Anal oral cozier'. It was time to pull my finger out.

"I hired a car especially," I told Ana Zorrilla, hoping to push her eco buttons. "Probably could've taken the bus but so what, yeah?"

"Well, we all drive in the States," replied Zorrilla in rather disappointingly friendly style. She didn't berate me using words like 'emissions' or 'socio-economic'. She wasn't wearing any wicker, either. Not even hemp, which is a sort of poor man's wicker. Zorrilla led me to an office past beaming reception staff. Calming music was being piped through, there were signs in Braille, the walls were brightly coloured – that was if you could see them for all the drawings and posters done by children of their pets. I could just make out the yelps and whines of rescued pets in the background. There wasn't even a whiff of wee.

"You'd like to know about our role in helping to ban cockfighting?" said Zorrilla, as she sat down behind the desk.

"Mmm, yes please," I replied. She told me about the trips to court, committees, lawyers, the compromises over legislation – it was pretty dull stuff – until my ears pricked up. "I'd like to think the ban was brought in because of animal welfare but it's all about votes." She sounded slightly exasperated. "When the hurricane struck there was a great deal of attention on the animals that were left behind. So the national media focussed heavily on Louisiana and suggested that as a state we weren't doing enough for animal welfare. That coupled with people wanting to be re-elected meant a cockfighting ban was possible." She didn't seem entirely enthused by the success of the ban.

"It's going to go underground," she said matter-of-factly. "The conditions of the birds could worsen. That's what happened with dogfighting – people wouldn't take their dogs to the vet to get fixed, scared they would get caught."

"So what's the point of banning it, then? If it's legal at least it can be regulated."

"We can now educate people that it's wrong. It may take a lifetime but we can change attitudes."

Zorrilla was making sense. She was nothing like the gung-ho activist, who might demand people receive goats for Christmas instead of shiny gifts, that I had expected. I told her that I was planning to attend a cockfight during my stay.

"Okay," she said, looking concerned.

"What can I expect?"

"I've never been to a fight myself but colleagues have and they told me all about it. It's a very unpleasant sport done by unpleasant people. My predecessor had death threats from dogfighters, y'know?"

"Really? Do you expect death threats from cockfighters when

the ban comes into force?"

"I might be in a difficult position in the future."

"Gosh, that bad?"

"Well, this is the reality. You'll see young children baying for the blood of these animals, people provoking them to fight, a lot of blood and feathers and" – at this point Zorrilla made the 'icky' face which Americans have almost trademarked – "sucking the blood out of the chicken as some sort of ritual. I haven't seen it but that's what I was told."

"The picture you're painting is not getting any rosier," I offered.

"These are cruel people. You may see drugs, semi-automatic weapons, but…" Suffering a flashback to my pre-trip concerns for an awful second I thought the next word was going to be 'rape' so I interrupted Zorrilla, thanked her for her time and left. Yet for only a second I doubted whether it would be in the best interests of my future to carry on. This was what I came for. A gambling test in the face of emotional adversity. If people with a predilection for drugs and guns had to be involved, then so be it. There might even be some of those crack whores, too. The key went straight into the ignition.

Directions to the cockfight were pretty simple. Drive west for four hours and then turn right. The early-morning mist was refusing to budge so when heading out of the city on a road on stilts with swamp below, it felt like I was taking off toward a mash-potato sky, skimming the top of the trees as I went. It didn't last for long, however; the serene setting being replaced by the sort of freeway one sees on *World's Scariest Police Chases 6*, a show viewed mostly by people who have come back from a pub on a Friday night and are only fit to watch stolen cars spinning into lampposts, trucks and pedestrians. The carnage is briefly punctuated by the narrator, a retired police chief called, oh I don't know, Sheriff John McJustice, screaming "look at this idiot!", "out of control!" and "he's lost his mind!". Normally each sequence ends with McJustice blaring "the cops had to shoot him in the face!". With

McJustice's voice playing in my head, I focussed on not becoming just another statistic and after passing 12 McDonald's – yup, I counted 'em – it was time to make that right turn off Interstate 10. The Bayou Club, venue for the cockfight, was slap bang next to it. Handy for a quick getaway.

Dust filled the nose from a pot-holed car park. The roar of cars thundering by filled the ears. The Bayou Club was a wrought-iron shed. On its side was an eponymous neon sign. Each letter was securely fixed, apart from the B, which had come loose and was attempting to turn itself into the shape of an arse. All of the letters had neon strips tumbling out like liquorice in a candy store – red for strawberry, blue for blueberry and yellow for lemon. The setting was far from sweet. Across the road was a motel, gas station and – why not? – the Lucky Longhorn Casino. And that was it.

In the car park most of the characters I could see, apart from the obvious Texans, who all wore Stetsons, had either a baseball cap, hideous tattoo or goatee beard. If you had the full set did that make you some sort of leader? All, however, had an unmistakably ugly gait. Stooped, shoulders hunched up, their arms swinging way out in front of their bodies with palms facing in and fingers splayed as if to provide balance. And then the steps forward. Slow and deliberate, each leg passing the other like they had never been acquainted before rising up at right angles and thudding down to squash an imaginary bug.

I was beginning to stand out. I dialled the number of Tim, a member of the Louisiana Gamefowl Breeders' Association, who I had arranged to meet and guide me through my cockfighting experience. He had been a cockfighter for 20 years.

"I've been waylaid," he said. "I'll be wearing a brown shirt and short pants and have a lovely lady with me." I didn't think he needed to describe himself because I reckoned he would most certainly boast the 'full set', being a member and all. I was buoyed by Tim's cheery mood and felt slightly safer, although that didn't stop me from climbing back into the car when a group of four rednecks swung into the car park in a pick-up truck and eyed me like I was the freak. Tim had been vague and standoffish in telephone calls and emails prior to my visit, and I feared that he thought I was some Limey journalist trying to stitch him up with a scathing and right-on article about what a barbarian he and his sort were. The phone rang. Tim was in the Bayou Club shop. "There's a shop?" I scoffed.

Tim did not have the 'full set'. The closest he came to even one was a greying moustache. He was a roly-poly fellow, chubby-cheeked − rosy, too. He had brought his wife, Diane. The lovely lady. She was striking with dark, shoulder-length hair and a welcoming smile. "Edward, how are you?" said Tim with particular emphasis on 'you' as he reached out to shake my hand. "Diane spotted you and said it was you." "You stand out amongst all these rednecks, honey," she added. The shop − which sold t-shirts with the slogan 'we send our boys across the line to fight but we can't send our roosters across the line to fight − ain't that bullshit' − was crowded so Tim suggested "let's go across the road to the casino and gamble".

As Diane fed $100 bills into a Vegas-style poker console with a familiar loony tune, she told me about Tim and cockfighting.

"Tim's been doing it for as long as he's been doing it − shoot my luck's not in today − my kids love coming to the fights, I love it. We don't do anything − I wasn't expecting a jack there − we don't do anything to *make* these birds fight. It's a family event for us." In went another $100. "Everyone would bring the kids, the moms would cook up lots of food − I need a seven here."

Diane could talk. Perhaps the only thing that would stop her is if someone fed $100 in her slot. Tim read my mind. "Come on, I'll show you round."

We crossed the road and went back to the entrance to the Bayou Club where he started to tell me about courts, committees, lawyers and legislation. I had heard this before. Tim estimated that cockfighting was worth $300m a year to Louisiana, cursed that friends would lose their livelihoods and reminded me of the t-shirt in the shop, which was a reference to sending US troops to Iraq but making it a felony to transport roosters across state lines. He told me that when the ban is implemented he would have to slaughter 2,000 birds. "It doesn't make sense, Edward."

"What about the cruelty aspect, though?"

"You'll decide that for yourself today but let me tell you a story. An elderly neighbour of mine – sweet, sweet lady – told me, 'Your parents sent you to the best Christian school, you've got two degrees but you are involved in this cruel sport, goading these birds to kill.' So I gave her a hen and babies to look after. Within a few days she phoned me up, crying and hollering 'they're ripping each other to pieces!'. It's their nature, you gotta understand."

Every so often our chat was interrupted by a 'full set' who welcomed Tim with a hearty handshake and asked him what the latest legal situation was. Each time the conversation would end the same way.

Tim, throwing his hands in the air, would squeal: "You a felon! You a felon!"

Full set: "God damn!"

I asked Tim how much gambling I could expect to see.

"Before the ban there were some big bets. Real big. In the thousands. In the Philippines they bet twenty or thirty thousand. But you won't see that. When the National Championship takes place here in May there'll be some big bets, too. But there could be a raid by the police at any time. Every time I come here I expect the police to bust us all for gambling."

"What would the legal situation be with that?" I asked.

"You a felon if you get caught three times! You a felon!"

"God damn!"

The talking had to stop. On with the action. Tim showed me through to the entrance of the Bayou Club, where we were greeted by a sweet-looking apple-pie of an old lady with round spectacles and shrivelled lips.

"You vouch for this young man?" she asked Tim.

"Sure do," he said, generously handing over my entrance fee, which was a steep $70.

"You're in good hands," she said and waved us through.

"You stick with me," said Tim. "They'll have spotters here looking for FBI, anyone suspicious, anyone that just doesn't look right."

"Do I look suspicious?"

Tim turned to look at his companion wearing white trainers, bell-bottom jeans and a blue t-shirt emblazoned with a mock image of the Pope listening to an iPod and the words 'I-Pope'. "You sure do."

When I entered the area of the club where the fighting would take place, I was taken aback at how organised and professional everything was. There were four stands – which must have gone 20 rows back – either side of a square ring, which was raised four feet in the air. Glass with 'No Gambling Allowed' stencilled on each side created a pen and bolted on top was a seven-foot cage, almost to the roof, and white-ish strip lighting. The pen was covered with dirt and two semi-circles – think of half of the Atomic Energy Commission logo – were drawn in what must have been whitewash. At the top of the West Stand – they were all labelled – sat a woman in a pink polo shirt, shouting into a microphone. "173 you got pick up, 35 you got pick up, pick up number 82, pick up!" Tim told me that these were the numbers of individual roosters who were ready for the pitter – the chap who would take the bird into the ring to fight – to take his brawler to be weighed.

Behind the East Stand and carrying on to the North was a blackboard with the name and number of every bird that would fight: 217 at this meet. Bear Claw, Coon Creek, Roof Rider Ellis, Hunter, Snake River, Tush Hog. After the name would be six squares for the scorers to write either a W or L. The bird which had six straight Ws would be declared the overall winner. "It'll go on to the early hours of tomorrow," said Tim. "The winner's owner will probably get about eighty thousand from a pot of a hundred thousand. I've had three or four good wins in derbies. In '98 in

Oklahoma I won about fifty. That put my kids through college."

With money like that involved it was proper that the carpet which covered the walkways underneath the stands was red. We walked on it until we were behind the West Stand, standing in front of four pens, separated by breeze blocks. They were painted white. The walls were white. They could have been stables but there were no doors or walls at the front. There was a ripe smell in the air, like disinfectant. "This is the drag," said Tim. "When the roosters have fought in the main arena they bring them here to finish the fight."

We trod the red carpet again to our seat high up in the West Stand. From our viewpoint I noticed that above each side of the cage were four television screens, showing pictures from each drag, which would allow spectators to follow previous fights.

Diane rejoined us after her stint in the casino. She sat next to me. "Were you lucky in the Longhorn?" I quizzed.

"Not lucky honey," she said. "Lost about two hundred but I did win a place in the draw for a pick-up."

The national anthem played, we all stood to attention and when the music stopped, the mayhem began. Two men entered the arena, each with a rooster under their arm. Holding on to the birds' sides, they placed them on the dirt and allowed them to stretch their legs in that recognisable high-kicking chicken style. Then they tucked them back under an arm, strode towards the centre and stood opposite each other slightly chest-on. The birds became manic, trying to peck each other's eyes, only succeeding in tearing feathers from their foe. They were to be the first of many to fly. That was just the warm-up, however. Placing their birds on the dirt once more, the pitters, on their haunches as if lighting a rocket, held the bird with thumbs and forefingers by the tail feathers. Then they let go. It was as though two Roman candles had been lit. The squawking, screaming birds whirred towards each other in a blur of colour. Reds, golds, yellows, blues and blacks flew through the air with the glint of razor-blade steel catching the eye. It was the most lethal fireworks show I'd ever seen.

This happened two or three more times before the fight was banished to the drag. Two more birds were brought in and then they too went to the drag. From here on it was a just a procession of feathered psychos. One fight after another. Despite the violence, the drip-drip of a new fight every couple of minutes allowed one to get complacent. Soon there was a feeling of 'seen it all before'.

Diane certainly had. She amused herself by filling me in with all the family news – "my son would've come today but he's babysitting my father-in-law's dog" – and telling me how they would be up early to drive to Mississippi tomorrow for a family lunch and that she had baked goodies for all the babies – "we got a lot in our family".

Like an old pro, she would occasionally comment on the bedlam unfolding in front of us, particularly when I dared suggest a pitter was going through the 'ritual' of sucking a rooster's blood from his beak. "No silly, he's sucking the blood out so the bird can breathe." Otherwise, we moved on to other discussion points, notably the waistlines of some of the pitters. Diane displayed a wicked sense of humour.

"Sometimes you get a really fat guy," she chortled. "And you know what? He doesn't wear drawers. You can tell when he bends down to pick up the bird. Why would anyone do that? Butt-crack showing all over the place."

Like two old washer women, we gossiped away quite happily, with the fights a sideshow. "She didn't?" "She did!" "You're joking!" "I'm not!". Diane had juicier stuff than I. She told me how Roy Jones Junior, a former 'boxer of the decade', used to fight roosters at Sunset, a pit not far from the Bayou Club. And (this is good) that she used to babysit Britney Spears because she was best of friends with her mom at high school. Surely she would divulge the dirt on troubled Britney?

"Good people, bad choices. That's all I'm going to say about that."

The few seconds of silence that followed between us were like a challenge that Diane could not pass up, however. She soon spilled the real reason behind Britney's high-profile 'breakdown'. I'd love to share it with you but I fear that lawyers would come at me like one of the crazed cocks. Suffice to say I could sell the story to a tabloid newspaper tomorrow for a greater sum than was on offer for the winning rooster. But I was there to make money gambling on cockfighting, not celebrity tittle-tattle, something I had completely forgotten about while chatting with Diane.

"Is there much gambling going on?" I asked Tim.

"Sure is," he said. "You hear that? Someone just shouted 'couple hundred across'. That means he wants to bet on the rooster across the other side of the pit. And that Texan down there is taking lots of bets." Tim pointed out a 6ft 5in Texan in a Stetson with a black droopy moustache and chiselled jaw. He looked like someone you didn't want to owe money to.

I knew I had transposed into the culture when, without a trace of a pun, I turned to Tim, all 14 stone of him with forearms capable of bending the bars of the cage in front, and said: "What's better, a big cock or a little cock?"

"I don't think it matters a great deal, Edward."

"Okay," I mused. "So how do I know which bird to bet on? Have we got any form?"

"No," said Tim. "People bet because of the pitter... just like people back horses because of a trainer."

"We got $200 on number 59," squealed Diane.

"That's right," said Tim. "The pitter's a friend, I know he looks after his birds."

With the "couple a hundred across" cries intensifying I reasoned that this was about as good a recommendation as I would get, so I squeezed past Tim and Diane to make the acquaintance of with the Texan in the Stetson.

"No gambling allowed," cried the lady in the pink polo shirt over the microphone. "No gambling allowed, so you, um, need to, er, control that." It was hardly the stinging rebuke that was going to stop this crowd and it certainly wasn't going to stop me.

I had travelled thousands of miles to strike a bet and like every journey begins with the smallest step, mine would come to an end with the dozen or so between me and the Texan in the Stetson. They were tentative ones – this was criminal after all. But the welfare of the animals was not given a second thought and the potential emotional triggers that were the Katrina tour, Sean 'I'm still off it' Kamplinski and the stark warnings of Ana Zorrilla, which had threatened to turn me into a blubbing mess, were even more distant. I was purely concentrating on getting my money into the hand of the Texan in the Stetson. It was all I needed to achieve. Suddenly I felt the whole crowd peering at me. The skinny Englishman was gambling. As I walked my jeans began to stick to my thighs, the pores fired into action by the dollars burning in my pocket. My mouth went dry, swabbed of moisture by one of a thousand feathers floating in the air.

"A couple hundred on number 59," I mumbled to the Texan in the Stetson, handing him a hot, sweaty roll. He didn't even look at me as he returned a slip recording the bet. I was on. An illegal wager. Piano-wire nerves slackened and a weird sense of peacefulness washed over. I let out a sigh of relief and instead of sitting on the edge of my seat as the fight began, I sat back in it. Despite having seen about 20 or 30 fights up until that point, I was unaware of whether No 59, of unremarkable black and red plume, was defeating its rival, a considerably snazzier gold colour with a crimson crown, or not. The birds were getting tangled together an awful lot by virtue of the blades on their legs. I looked to Tim for a cue. He looked agitated. Maybe it wasn't going so well.

"We're going to the drag!" piped Diane unexpectedly. They certainly were. Tim and Diane leapt from their seats and hurried off down the steps. I followed.

The drag was full of bodies bobbing and weaving, trying to sneak a better peek at one of the four fights which were continuing. The smell of disinfectant had been replaced by something sweeter. Raw, rank and cooling the nostrils, it was the smell of blood and death. The white walls and breeze blocks had red smears. The floor was pockmarked with the same colour. A large oil drum was in the corner. At the bottom were two dead birds. There was no pang of regret that I had just gambled on a fight which would result in one of the birds joining them. There was no pang of anything come to think of it. I had been subdued, wrongly thinking that all I needed to do to prove myself was hand over the money. I had to engender a stomach for the fight otherwise it meant nothing. I wanted to feel nervous, excited and tense – how I had felt a thousand times before when watching a bet.

Diane pushed me to the front of the mob to get a better view of No 59's battle to the death. Tim was shouting instructions to his pitter friend, who was tall and rangy and wearing a green t-shirt and green baseball cap. His eyes were wide and his face gaunt. He remained expressionless throughout. Occasionally he would thrust his hips forward and throw out a leg at right angles to mimic the slashing, kicking action of his rooster. My No 59 was winning; all shield and rapier to his opponent's lumpen thrusts. I stood with arms folded. I couldn't raise a whimper in support of my bird, until something caught my eye.

"Hey," I said to Diane, pointing to No 59's fair-feathered adversary. "His head was red but now it has turned black. What's going on?"

"That's 'cos he's dying. He's bleeding to death."

Indeed. He looked well-beaten. The duel appeared a formality. If the bird did not peck back at No 59 during three counts to ten and then one long count of 20, then I would have my first winner at a cockfight. But this rooster would not give in. Despite being about to greet his maker, again and again he launched his beak forward. Something began to stir within me. During one count he even managed a fully-fledged attack, much to the amazement of the more experienced watchers. My hands moved to my hips, and my head moved from side to side to get a better view.

"They're mean, mean, mean," said Diane. "They just want to

fight and kill."

Mercifully, we were not far from the 20 count. The blood had seeped from the rooster's perforated arteries and barring recovery, the bout was over. 16… 17… 18… 19… 20… To my surprise I clenched my fists and gave it some mini pump, accompanied with a "yes!" under my breath. Ah ha! It made sense now. When No 59's opponent briefly hit back, the prospect of a losing wager arose. It had motivated me. I suppose the thought of victory did not have the same upshot because I believed that I had already 'won' by placing the bet in the first place. The gambler had finally come to the fore only when the prospect of being a couple of hundred poorer arose. It is a feeling with which every punter is familiar. Win and live, lose and die that will never change.

Tim's pitter pal picked up No 59, put it under his arm and walked off with the same expressionless face. His bird, beadily eyeing the throng, would fight again. The black and bloodied head of his dead combatant lolled to the side in time with his pitter's heavy steps, dripping its juice on to the floor and leaving a trail across each of my white trainers.

To make sure that this sight had not altered my stoicism I had two more bets, one winner and a loser to unofficially become a felon of the US – although I suppose if the governor of Louisiana ever reads these words it could become official – and perhaps the first person to admonish a losing bird with a disdainful "what a cock!". Tim and Diane saw me to the exit. The fight would continue until the early hours. They had been wonderful hosts. They had paid for my entrance, bought me lunch and were desperate for me to understand the nuances of a sport they were passionate about. They were not "unpleasant" people. That much was clear from warm smiles. I had seen no semi-automatic weapons, drugs or young children baying for blood like Ana Zorrilla had suggested.

"I hope you are able to see our side of things," said Tim. "Not many people listen to us, I've done so many interviews…"

"He went to one in a suit and tie once," interrupted Diane.

"They make us look like fools," finished Tim.

Outside the Bayou Club it was nightfall. I had been in there almost six hours. On my drive back to New Orleans I pondered how I had been able to gamble on a sport for which a creature would die for my punting pleasure and that I felt not in the least bit shameful. Was it because I grew up in the English countryside and foxhunting was part of my culture? Was it because they were 'only birds' hell bent on killing? Or was it because I didn't lose? Yes to all three and you can make your own moral judgements. But there was a more emphatic 'yes' to a fourth question: hasn't Louisiana and New Orleans got bigger problems to deal with first rather than wasting its police and justice system to enforce a ban on cockfighting? The crime, the drugs, the homeless, the chaos of Katrina.

Next day I was loading my bags into the back of a cab to take me to the airport, still wearing trainers which had picked up a couple of spots of blood which had changed from red to black overnight. I was convinced my judgement was correct, especially when I heard a familiar soft-shoe shuffle across the street. It was Kamplinski making his daily pilgrimage to the Mississippi. He looked up, waved and shouted: "I'm back on it, Pete!"

Chapter 13

Luck – Glasgow

Almost four years to the day that I began my gambling adventure around the globe, I was back outside the Ladbrokes in Paddington station where it all began. But I was not there to have a bet. I had been walking past it regularly the past few months to visit genuine bloodsuckers at St Mary's hospital, who had drained enough blood from my veins to keep Count Dracula energised for a clubbing trip to Ibiza. He wanted to get some colour in his cheeks.

Soon after returning from Australia I developed perpetual cold and 'flu' symptoms. I would soak the sheets at night through sweat, have a constant runny or stuffed nose, a sore throat and feel generally lethargic. Consistent was a cough, which would just not go away. Sometimes it was a tickly one, other times it sounded like a trombone with a sock stuffed down the front. But always, always it would be accompanied by a strange kaleidoscopic goo. If I moved too quickly, or turned over in bed at night, I could hear the goo groaning around in my lungs. It was a popular party trick; reaching up high with my right hand and then bending over to the left to produce a sound like a cow being poked with a stick. You know that slime that Noel Edmonds used to enjoy dropping on unsuspecting celebrities' heads in TV game shows in the 1990s? That was an afternoon's work for me.

Well, the doctors were fascinated. I was a sort of celebrity at St Mary's. I knew all the nurses by name, who would shove needles in my arm and fill pot after multicoloured pot of my mauvey blood. Sometimes I would cough up some of my famed goo for them. Red ones, yellow ones, blues and greens.

My doctor was an awfully goofy chap from Sri Lanka. He was gobsmackingly intelligent and had gone to Cambridge, or the other one, before specialising in immunology. Typically of super brainy people, he lacked any sense of style and would always shuffle in to see me in the same tatty blue suit, his trousers failing to cover his ankles.

So clever was he that often he would just bang on and on in this medical mumbo-jumbo, drawing complex diagrams or jotting equations. I couldn't understand what he was going on about. Sensing this he would instead talk about cricket, in particular Sri Lanka spinner Muttiah Muralitharan, who had since passed Shane Warne's world record wicket-haul.

Rather worryingly, though, he didn't know what was wrong. I would visit every month and he would insist on asking the same questions, which rather gave away that he thought I must have been either sharing a needle with half of London or sleeping with them. Or both.

"'Fraid not, Doc," I'd say. "My only vice is gambling."

I suggested that my illness might have been contracted by refusing to wash the snot and saliva of Desert Orchid from my palm 20 years ago. "Are you sure you're not a drug user?" was his reply.

I felt rather pleased with myself for baffling someone who was infinitely cleverer than I. He even went to a conference in Brussels to discuss my case with other doctors in ill-fitting blue suits. On his return he decided that my immune system was exactly like the Wigan Athletic defence. It had gaping holes in it and it didn't matter what anyone tried to do to improve it, it would always be that way.

So I was stuck with a permanent cold and a dirty cough which proved far more effective at making people turn up their noses at me than "I'm a gambler, you know" had ever been.

The Doc told me that about one in a million people in the UK had a puzzling fault with their immune system. But there were one in four million with a fault which just could not be fixed. Well, that was crushing news. I was a four million to one shot. All my life I had been searching to land massive life-changing odds, and, until that point, I had been unaware that they were staring back at me every time I looked in the mirror. That is what I call unlucky.

Rightly or wrongly, I reckoned that if I was a walking, talking four million to one chance then it shouldn't be beyond me to land similar odds. I was due for a bit of luck.

While waiting for the Doc to turn up one morning, I chanced upon an article in one of those grubby waiting room magazines (the amount of germs on those, by the way, may one day be responsible for a new plague) about a bingo hall in Glasgow which had, in the space of 21 days, two £1m winners.

There could be only one place, then, to try my fortune. I booked myself on the next available train, making sure it was not an Old Firm football weekend (did you know the number of violent crimes in the city increase by more than 100 per cent on the weekend of the fixture?). Then all I would have to do to win a sizeable sum was be faster with an oversize marker pen than a boozed-up Scottish widow. I wasn't that frail – yet. Besides, with my hacking, wheezing and stories about what a terrible ailment I had, I would fit right in.

Between 1960 and 1985 the Church of England was reduced to almost half its previous size. The Swinging Sixties, free love, The Beatles, women's lib and, a little later, Luke Skywalker and Darth Vader could all share a proportion of responsibility. I 'blame' bingo. There has been much hand-wringing and pontificating – some seriously hefty volumes have been written – about the decline in religion during that period but none picked up on the apparent preference for folks to set eyes down on a bingo card rather than their feet in some damp church.

Consider this: by 1963, when the rot had set in for the Bible bashers, the bingo industry boasted more than 14 million members and three years later a Gallup poll reported that almost a quarter of the country had enjoyed a game in the previous 12 months. The Church was losing 30,000 supporters a year while bingo boomed. Paradoxically – you'll like this bit – while people lost faith in a supreme being, there was a rise in the numbers of those who started to believe in lucky charms and the unfortunate properties of number 13.

Bingo, or Housey-Housey as it was back then, was blindingly glitzy. The likes of Cilla Black, Diana Dors and Tommy Steele would mingle with the punters at the local hall, listening intently for the numbers to be called by a man in a sparkly jacket with a penchant for sexual innuendo: 18 – coming of age, 43 – down on your knees, 56 – was she worth it?, a call said to have derived from the cost of a lady of the Portsmouth night.

I didn't expect much glam when I arrived at The Forge Mecca bingo hall in Parkhead, a long punt downfield from the Celtic football stadium. The 20-minute taxi ride had taken 10 as my driver – Elmohamady – seemed intent on killing us both. Perhaps he had misunderstood my request of 'take me to Mecca', and thought he had better put his foot down. On a circuitous route he would accelerate and then brake suddenly on icy roads, sending us skidding toward first a gritter truck and then an old lady pushing a supermarket trolley full of newspapers, all the time squealing "woop, woop! This is wicked innit?".

He ceased after a chilly rebuke reminding him that his *raison d'être* as a cab driver was to make sure he got paid and there was very little likelihood of that if both of us were wrapped around a lamppost. This seemed to be some sort of epiphany to him but I liked his chutzpah so I booked him to collect me once my bingo exploits had finished. Besides, with temperatures predicted to plunge to minus seven, I would have little hope of finding another cab.

The Forge did not look worth the risk of Elmohamady's

driving. From the outside it was everything the 60s were not. A charmless identikit building from every retail park you have ever seen. It could have been a DIY store or electrical outlet. Cilla Black? Jimmy Crankie wouldn't be seen dead there.

I approached the girl at the reception and asked to see Alistair, the manager, who was expecting me. No words came out. An unfortunate effect of my immune system shutdown was that in particularly cold weather, the gunk and gunge had a tendency to congeal and then, well, sort of freeze around my vocal cords meaning that I had a habit of sounding a lot like a faulty air conditioning unit in a one-star apartment in Magaluf. Only a hearty hack would budge it – the sort of sound a camel might make if regurgitating an oboe – so I let out an undignified "aach-aach-ung-splatter" and disposed of the offending sputum in a handkerchief.

"This it, git it up sonnie, does use gid," said a woman whose face, presumably once vulnerable and fresh, had been spotted by the harsh Glasgow winter which thought 'right, we'll have you'. "Jus use makes sure use don make a sound like tha when I'm playin' in there, o-key?" I was fitting right in.

Alistair, the manager, soon greeted me. He was surprisingly young – I had expected someone as old and as weather-beaten as my new friend – but he was reassuringly Scottish. "A've had a burst water pipe today, four or five inches a water, tiles falling off… it's been absolute MUR-DA."

We went up to his office to talk. An empty packet of Walker's crisps and a can of Irn Bru lay on the desk and I could make out the faint calls of a game in progress below. "Number seven… on its own … number seven." It became apparent that my chances of a £1m win, and your hopes, dear reader, of a Hollywood-style ending to this book, had been dashed when he told me that I was only the 74th person to venture out on such a bitter night. I presumed that Elmohamady and his chums might have accounted for another 30 or so in cab prangs around the city, but even so, with bingo winnings inextricably linked to the number of players, Alistair told me the most I could hope for was "a hundred quid".

Moving on, I pressed him for details of the two £1m winners who had earned The Forge the "luckiest hall in Britain tag". At 2,500 seats it was also the biggest. You can't be one without the other. Both wins had occurred within weeks of each other in September 2007. Margaret Shearer, who claimed she knew something big would happen because she'd had a hot flush, became Britain's first bingo millionaire. She also carried a miniature Buddha in her handbag and her regular partner was her mum, whose surname was Money.

"She still plays," said Alistair.

"Is she here tonight?"

"No."

The second millionaire was Jean McCullagh. Hers was a depressing story. Almost immediately upon receiving the loot, she became involved in a legal battle with her sisters-in-law, who claimed she had promised to share any winnings.

"Not sure they still come," said Alistair. "I know one out of the three who was disputing it has died now, but, erm, the other two I don't think they talk right enough."

We moved on to discuss the general workings of the club, which provided an interesting character profile of the bingo player. "They like their prize money, they like things for free and they like you to know it. To get people in during the cold weather we've offered free chips, free chips 'n' gravy, free chips 'n' curry. Oh, and free tea. They're never happy with the prizes on offer. You'll be about to announce that night's winnings and before you've even had a chance to tell 'em, they've shouted 'get the money up!'."

I tended to agree. However, armed with a rather fetching pink dabber to cancel out my numbers, I was soon in position in the hall to, hopefully, win a jackpot which would pay for my train fare. Alistair started to explain the 'rules' but I wasn't listening. I mean, how hard could it be? Someone shouts the numbers, you dab them out on your card. Instead I was focussing on my fellow players. The majority seemed not long for this world or, if you will, their number would soon be up. I fancied that my sharper reflexes and hearing had to give me a better chance.

I was hopeless. I couldn't find the numbers quick enough. By the time I had dabbed one, the caller was two ahead by which time I was fretting over whether this was the first sign of some sort of degenerative brain disease. I was a disaster at bingo, a game so mundane that professional morons like Kerry Katona, that bastion of ignorance, claimed to enjoy and succeed at it. Forget Melbourne, horrible losses and pooing myself in public, this was the definitive low point.

The look on my face as I vainly searched for the correct digits was the same your senile grandma has when, increasingly desperate, she cries 'where's Millie the cat... I can't see her... I've lost her... I...' before a relative chirps in with 'Grandma, Millie died a long time ago, remember?' In this instance, the 'relative' was Alistair. "Er, Ed? The numbers are ordered by rows – singles, teens, twenties, thirties and so on. It's quite simple, yeah?"

Yes, it was quite simple. With the knowledge absorbed and my tongue lolling out of the corner of my mouth, I punched off the numbers with increasing ferocity. I was away. There was the occasional grunt of triumph, too, as I nailed another number thanks to the hearing of a barn owl. Faster and faster I seemed to progress, spending the seconds in between calls muttering 'give-it-to-me-give-it-to-me', and just as glory was upon me, with only two numbers remaining for 'house', some small, ancient ball of knitwear in the corner would let out a meek "meh". That's not even a shout of house for Christ's sake! She should be disqualified! It sounded like vowels! Alistair, officiate here!

Then a new round would start and once more I would be engrossed. I was smashing the dabber into the table now. The grunts were getting louder. More aggressive. Real lowest common denominator stuff. In between calls I took to eyeing the other players, pointing at them with my dabber while mouthing 'this is my game now – the new breed's in town' and 'time's up grandma!' And, disturbingly, imagining jabbing the dabber hard on the forehead of a previous foe to leave a perfect pink circle.

I had, of course, taken things too far and failed to realise that the whole point of bingo is that no matter who you are, or what super powers you might think you have in relation to the others in the hall, you cannot possibly improve your chances of victory. In that regard bingo is rather a cruel form of wagering because you believe the opposite. Whereas with a football bet or horse punt you can see with your own eyes that the game is up when your team is 2-0 down or your nag has been put to sleep a few furlongs from home, with bingo you always think you are on the cusp of triumph only for it to be snatched away from you by someone smelling of wee. There's a moral in there somewhere.

So I didn't become a millionaire. Nor a hundredaire (is that a word?). The final ignominy was left for the caller to deliver, who wandered over after the final number. "I saw you were struggling at first," said LeighAnne, "so I slowed down for you."

If I'm being honest, the game is up when you go to a bingo hall hoping to win a fortune. It wasn't a low point at all. That much was confirmed the next day when I went to visit a Gamblers Anonymous fellowship to the north of a city centre frozen solid. Throughout this tale I have dipped a toe cautiously into the think tank about addiction, unsure because I didn't know enough about the subject. I was no addict yet but was conscious that it was a subject which needed to be broached, at least for the sake of journalistic balance. Also, I didn't want to be accused of glamorising gambling. Sure, for me it has been all rips and giggles but there are always those who can't handle the losses.

This was the end of my journey and, undoubtedly, I had failed in a bid to prove myself capable of earning a living as a sporting chancer. Indeed, I was even pleased at the prospect of a prolonged betting break. Addicts, this much I do know, don't think like that. So how do they think?

Tommy, a reformed addict, had the answer. His story was a humbling one. It made an impact, too. It confirmed to me that winning at gambling is not all about the monetary gain. If you can enjoy it as a hobby, make the most of that flash of adrenalin when placing a bet, the even greater rush when it is running and treat success and failure with even-handedness, then you are a winner. During the course of this tale I might have broken most of the rules of the gambling book when betting drunk, uninitiated, to chase losses or with money I just plain didn't have, but at least I'd had a good time. That is success of a sort. Faced with a tale as harrowing as Tommy's and the losses – not just financial – he has had to endure, it is certainly not a defeat. Defeat would have been to have fallen into gambling's unrelenting clutches.

I met Tommy on the morning before catching a train back to London. He was around 5ft 6in, had a white, closely-trimmed beard and small dark eyes. In a Scots accent harsher than the sound of grit being crunched on the streets outside, he welcomed me warmly and showed me around the GA office: woodchip wallpaper, damp bruised walls, a sink, pamphlets and literature, a poem pinned up called 'I am Addiction'.

For an hour he talked, rarely looking directly at me. Eyes down. Or preferring to peer through the caged window at black tower blocks forming bars across the horizon. We stood together, arms folded, huddled by the electric heater; him with a smoker's cough and me with my wretched constitution, grumbling and wheezing together. He stopped only occasionally, to make a cup of tea, answer the phone or roll a cigarette. Sometimes he needed prompting for more details but otherwise I just listened, infrequently offering impotent platitudes like "gosh", "blimey" and "really?". So I've reproduced his words here in full.

"I don't gamble anymore but we believe you are never cured but it can get arrested on a daily basis. I get a reprieve on a daily basis so long as I keep doing what I am doing. If I severed my contact with GA I wouldn't go back gambling straight away but I'd gradually slip down and down and down. You see I'm the problem. My head would eventually take me back to where I was.

"And if it wasn't gambling it would be something else. In my experience addicts are people unfortunate enough to have addictive personalities. Drugs, drink, gambling, smoking or whatever addicts will find something else to get addicted to. I'm addicted to smoking. As soon as I said that I want a smoke [laughs]. I'm addicted, I know that. I am addicted to alcohol. Not had a drink for 30 years.

"When I started gambling, I loved gambling. It was the buzz, the excitement. But in the last two or three years I hated it but I just couldn't stop, I couldn't stop.

"I started gambling at 15. The bookmakers lived above me, in a tenement. They didn't have shops. It used to be that the bookies were at street corners. What always amazed me was there were quite a few one-legged street corner bookies. I used to wonder about that? It didnae dawn on me till a few years later. People lost legs during the war and couldnae find employment so took up bookieing. Amazing.

"I remember my first bet very, very clearly. I bet a horse which probably no-one will remember now, a horse called Papa Fourway. It was a flat horse, it was unbeaten and it was always odds on. Ten pound on to win a pound. I had a friend, he was a couple of years older than me, and he always had a wallet, which was unknown in those days, and he worked in the city and he used to change his money at the banks into ten shilling notes so his wallet looked fat 'n' all crispy. And I was overawed by this wallet. He told me he'd got it from gambling but he didnae. He worked in a warehouse and he was blagging shoes and selling them. He introduced me to Papa Fourway.

"At the time I was a message boy for a grocer and I stole everything I could, everything that wasn't nailed down I stole so I could bet this horse. My next bet was a big race and my horse won at 12-1. I had two pounds on it, got 26 back and that was a fortune to me. I was hooked. I was hooked by a winner. Totally. Right up until the day I came to GA.

"My father died when I was 15. He wasn't a compulsive

gambler but he bet every day and it was coppers. He used to come up and listen to the races on the radio and I'd listen along with him. Maybe I was eight or nine. And I was always concerned that his horse wasn't mentioned and he'd say 'that's ok, that's ok'. Other times it might win and I was really excited about that.

"And there was a lady, a widow, a mad lady, who stayed at the top of our street. Aggie was her name, a fiery mop of red hair and she would gamble on two flies going up the window pane. So four or five of us kids would go to her house and play cards. We used to win a lot off her, we cheated like hell. She was compulsive. She couldnae stop. We were in there regular playing cards. It was always a big thing, 'how are we gonna get money to go to Aggies?' They were exciting days. When I loved to gamble.

"I thank God that I'm not doing it today because of these things [points at a computer] and credit cards. When I stopped there were no credit cards. I stopped at 31. I'm 71 now. I was in the hands of an unlicensed money lender and I stayed in his grip up until a year before I came into GA. The only reason I got out of his clutches was that he died. If you didnae pay in time you pay very high interest. If you didnae pay at all you get your legs cut off. So you borrow more money to pay on time, keep going back and back and back.

"So I had to find other sources so stealing came into it a lot, borrowin' came into it a lot. I ended up in prison for attempted murder and I did four years. It wasn't freak. It was deliberate. I'd been assaulted. Two guys came up behind me. One stabbed me in the back. I don't know why they did it. I had a reputation in those days for being violent. A week later I knew where they were in the boozers and I hit one with a very heavy domino board. A lad and his brother. I sliced the other guy's leg. The only reason it was his leg was that he put his leg up to protect himself and his arms were up protecting his face. With what? Oh, I, er, I took a knife. So I wasn't a very nice guy. Believe me. Today I wouldn't stand on a fly or a beetle. I've become very, very different.

"You see you probably wouldn't understand about gamblers...

you probably don't know anything about gamblers… see, I had a three-course meal before I left the house in the morning. The first course was self pity. I had to find someone to blame. And I could not. So the second course was resentment. I could find it anywhere. By the time I was ready to go through the door the third course was ready and that was hate. I hated everything and everybody. I hated good guys, bad guys. I hated good guys worse than bad guys 'cos they showed me up for what I was. I walked about in a constant rage for years and years and years.

"The day I had my last bet I worked in a factory and I had holiday pay and bonus pay to collect. It was quite a lot of money. And I sat with the social worker and my wife till one in the morning and I was on the six to two shift the next morning. And that was the day I was to collect all the money. I promised the social worker, I promised my wife, I promised myself. I'd come straight home. I wouldn't do it. I'd come straight home because I'd been through six weeks when I'd gambled every penny and lost every penny. I was destitute.

"I came out of work that day at two, you got paid in cash in those days, and I started to walk home. It was a nice summer's day, the 14th of July 1971. I walked along about five miles and if I kept going in the direction I was going, I wouldn't have seen a bookies at all but I veered in through the housing scheme … into the bookies … two bets… skint … broke. And that was the worst and best day of my life because that was the day I contacted GA.

"I haven't had a bet since. My 40th year. So people say to me today coming on 40 years 'why do you still come?'. The answer I give them is that I had nothing to lose, I'd lost it all and today I've got so much to lose. I don't want to risk it."

After leaving Tommy I made my way back to Glasgow Central station where I spotted a Ladbrokes. What a nice symmetry, I thought, if I could end my jaunt as it began, with a dog bet at a Ladbrokes at a rail terminus. Golly, it might even win. But then I remembered that first bet had lost. And I remembered my pitiable record betting on greyhounds. I looked through the window of the shop and saw a rail worker in a fluorescent jacket grimly feeding coins into a slot machine, one man, ashen-faced and nervous, switching glances from television screen to the form guide in his hand, and another, patently penniless, struggling with possessions in a carrier bag, counting out pennies on to the cash desk with grubby, fingerless gloves. I didn't go in. It was time to go home.

)